THE OFFICIAL CARRY ON FACTS, FIGURES & STATISTICS

THE OFFICIAL CARRY ON FACTS, FIGURES & STATISTICS

A COMPLETE STATISTICAL ANALYSIS OF THE CARRY ONS

BY KEVIN SNELGROVE

FOREWORDS BY
ALAN HUME AND JACK DOUGLAS

APEX PUBLISHING LTD

First published in 2008, updated and reprinted in 2009 by
Apex Publishing Ltd
PO Box 7086, Clacton on Sea, Essex, CO15 5WN, England

www.apexpublishing.co.uk

British Library Cataloguing-in-Publication Data
A catalogue record for this book
is available from the British Library

ISBN 1-906358-09-5   978-1-906358-09-9

Typeset in 10.5pt Arial Narrow

Cover Design: Siobhan Smith
Photograph © ITV plc (Granada International)

Printed and bound in Great Britain By
the MPG Books Group, Bodmin and King's Lynn

Dedicated to:
Bernard Bresslaw, Peter Butterworth, Kenneth Connor, Jack Douglas, Charles Hawtrey, Hattie Jacques, Sid James, Peter Rogers, Patsy Rowlands, Terry Scott, Joan Sims, Gerald Thomas and Kenneth Williams.

In memory of Doris Ethel Snelgrove
07/09/1911 – 01/06/2000

CONTENTS

The entrance to Pinewood studios, the home of the Carry Ons

ACKNOWLEDGEMENTS

For their support and contributions a very special thank you to the following:

Holly Aird, Terence Alexander, Lynda Baron, Liz Bresslaw, Jackie Bright, Morris Bright, Dora Bryan OBE, Paul Burton, Peter Byrne, Mark Campbell, Gerald Campion, David Claydon, Kenneth Cope, Chris Cowlin, Alan Curtis, Alexandra Dane, Larry Dann, Ed Deveraux, Jack Douglas, Patrick Durkin, Shirley Eaton, Heather Emmanuel, Hilda Fenemore, Harry Fielder, Fenella Fielding, Liz Fraser, Hugh Futcher, Sally Geeson, Peter Gilmore, Mike Grady, David Graham, Angela Grant, Leon Greene, Anita Harris, Melvyn Hayes, Norman Hudis, Alan Hume, Laraine Humphreys, Oscar James, Sue James, Valerie James, Vivienne Johnson, Anna Karen, Carol Kenyon, Charlotte Kinsler, Samuel Kinsler, Rosalind Knight, Burt Kwouk, Barry Langford, Marjie Lawrence, Dilys Laye, Valerie Leon, Maureen Lipman, Natalie May, Albert Moses, Don McCorkindale, Desmond McNamara, Janet Moat, Arshad Naheed, Andrew Newlyn, Richard O'Brien, Richard O'Callaghan, Milo O'Shea, Christine Ozanne, Nicholas Parsons OBE, Bill Pertwee, Jacki Piper, Nigel Planer, Nosher Powell, Jean Prior, Terry Prior, Linda Regan, Kate Robbins, Ken Rock, Anton Rodgers, Peter Rogers, Robert Ross, Tina Rowe, Ann Runeckles, Steve Saville, Darren Senior, Valerie Shute, Sir Donald Sinden CBE, Marc Sinden, Audrey Skinner, Michelle Skinner, Madeline Smith, Julie Snelgrove, Kate Snelgrove, Samantha Snelgrove, Philip Steele, Ronnie Stevens, Marianne Stone, Philip Stone, Christine Sutch, Frank Thornton, Harry Towb, Wanda Ventham, Valerie Van Ost, Richard Webber, Ken Whitehead, Richard Wilson and June Whitfield CBE.

And to Rob Milburn at **www.thewhippitinn.com** for use of photographs on pages 36, 103 and 119.

An extra special thank you to Peter Rogers and ITV plc (Granada Ventures) for the use of the Carry On name.

FOREWORD
BY ALAN HUME

It is a great pleasure to have been asked to write the foreword for *The Official Carry On Facts, Figures & Statistics.*

Carry On and on and on for thirty productions, the most prolific series of feature film comedies from England or any other country. Not everybody's taste, but over 60% of filmgoers in the UK and other parts of the world loved them.

The producer Peter Rogers masterminded every script, and also the casting of the artists, who were wonderfully talented actors.

Peter's director Gerald Thomas was an expert director and very talented film editor. His expertise got the utmost out of each script, his editing and direction giving the actors every opportunity to get as much fun and laughter over to the audience as possible.

Peter Rogers and Gerald Thomas were a very strong team. None of these thirty Carry On films were ever over schedule or over budget, a unique achievement in the unpredictable business of film production.

I was lucky enough to work as a cameraman on sixteen Carry On films, every day was a pleasure to be there, and it was the happiest, funniest film set I ever worked on. Often there would be hilarious laughter behind the camera at the antics going on in front of it.

One such incident I found not quite so amusing was when I allowed Charles Hawtrey to ride my Lambretta around the car park for a shot in *Carry On Cabby* (1963). Charles was no rider or driver and in trying to negotiate the way around parked cars he managed to run my Lambretta into my parked car, denting both in one go. Fortunately he was unscathed. So once again a Carry On was completed on schedule and on budget.

Enjoy these interesting statistics from the famous Carry Ons ...

Alan Hume
(Cameraman on 16 Carry On Films)

vii

FOREWORD
BY JACK DOUGLAS

It made my day when Kevin asked me to write the foreword to this book *The Official Carry On Facts, Figures & Statistics*. The highlight of my career was appearing in the Carry Ons. I did eight pictures spanning twenty-one years (1971-1992) - a big chunk of my life.

We could never have dreamt that the characters created in the films would still be popular some fifty years on. Our director Gerald Thomas was the best ever; the whole team were competent, professional and great fun to work with.

I feel that if anyone deserves a knighthood it is Peter Rogers for his contribution to the British film industry. In his ninetie's he still has his office at Pinewood Studios.

I still love watching the Carry Ons on television; they still make me laugh and long may it be so. Believe it or not the films were all made in the record time of six weeks. We all enjoyed them so much it was like playtime at school! Even though most of the team are gone now, they will live on forever on the screen.

Kevin has done a brilliant job compiling this book - rather him than me as what do I know about statistics? Other than 38-24-36 – tee hee!

I am sure this book will be successful, so read on, as we go into the studios, on the set, behind the camera and action.

So Carry On reading, I hope you enjoy the book.

Jack Douglas
(Appeared in eight Carry On films)

ABOUT THE CARRY ONS

For over fifty years the Carry Ons have been a part of the British way of life. The picture-postcard humour was brought to life way back in 1958 with *Carry On Sergeant*, a film scripted by Norman Hudis, produced by Peter Rogers and directed by Gerald Thomas. After the success of *Sergeant*, *Carry On Nurse* followed, which was to be a number one box office hit in 1959 and is a cult film today on the campus'es in the USA. Hudis went on to write another four films, *Teacher* (1959), *Constable* (1959), *Regardless* (1960) and *Cruising* (1962). In 1963 a new scriptwriter came on to the scene by the name of Talbot Rothwell, who started with *Cabby* (1963), and went on to write another nineteen films in the series, finishing with *Dick* in 1974. The Rogers and Thomas partnership averaged almost two films per year until the end of 1971. In this year *At Your Convenience* was released. It took almost five years for this film to make its money back. The Carry On films were starting to take a downward slide, which was resurrected in 1974 with *Dick* and almost peaked before its fall in 1976 with *England* and then finally in 1992 with *Columbus,* yet this film did make its money quickly. The Carry On films were finished for now! Yet Peter Rogers has said at a Carry On Convention that if a good enough script was written he would consider making another one, so they may not be finished.

In between the films a television programme was produced in 1969, *Carry On Christmas*. Another nineteen followed until the last programme in 1989, *Norbert Smith – A Life*. Though these were good they were never as popular as the films.

In 1973 *Carry On London*, the first of three stage shows, was performed at the Victoria Palace. This ran for a year and a half and starred many of the Carry On team that appeared in the films. The final stage show was *Wot a Carry On in Blackpool* and it ran for five months, though most of the team had now departed from this world to appear in the great Carry On in the sky. So the Carry Ons ended in 1992 with both the last film and the last stage show.

So Carry On gaining knowledge!

The home of the Carry Ons - Pinewood Studios

www.apexpublishing.co.uk

CHAPTER 1
THE FILMS

A-Z GUIDE

A is for Abroad (1972), *Again Doctor* (1969), *At Your Convenience* (1971),
            Again Christmas (1970) and *And in My Lady's Chamber* (1975)   = 5

B is for *Behind* (1975)   = 1

C is for *Cabby* (1963), *Camping* (1968), *Cleo* (1964), *Columbus* (1992),
            Constable (1959), *Cowboy* (1965), *Cruising* (1962),
            Christmas (1969), *Christmas* (1972), *Christmas* (1973)
            and *Christmas Classics* (1983)   = 11

D is for *Dick* (1974), *Doctor* (1967) and *Don't Lose Your Head* (1966) = 3

E is for *Emmannuelle* (1978) and *England* (1976)   = 2

F is for *Follow that Camel* (1967)   = 1

G is for *Girls* (1973)   = 1

H is for *Henry* (1970)   = 1

J is for *Jack* (1963)   = 1

L is for *Loving* (1970), *LampPosts of the Empire* (1975), *London*
            (1973/75) and *Laughing with The Slimming Factory* (1975)   = 4

M is for *Matron* (1971)   = 1

N is for *Nurse* (1958) and *Norbert Smith – A Life* (1989)   = 2

O is for *Orgy and Bess* (1975) and *One in the Eye for Harold* (1975) = 2

R is for *Regardless* (1960)   = 1

S is for *Sergeant* (1958), *Screaming* (1966), *Spying* (1964)
            and *Short Knights, Long Daze* (1975)   = 4

T is for *Teacher* (1959), *That's Carry On* (1977), *The Prisoner of Spenda*
            (1975), *The Baron Outlook* (1975), *The Sobbing Cavalier* (1975),
            The Nine Old Cobblers (1975), *The Case of the Screaming Winkles*
            (1975) and *The Case of the Coughing Parrot* (1975)   = 8

U is for *Up the Jungle* (1969), *Up the Khyber* (1968) and *Under the*
            Round Table (1975)   = 3

W is for *What a Carry On!* (1973), *Who Needs Kitchener?* (1975) and
            Wot a Carry On in Blackpool (1992)   = 3

DID YOU KNOW THE FOLLOWING?

The following five pages of bullet-pointed statistical information are facts from the Carry On's, so read on, it gets far more interesting from here on in ...

* Production on the Carry On films started on 24th March 1958 with *Sergeant*.

* It would cost £984,200 to make a Carry On film at today's prices – still very cheap.

* Most of the Carry On films were filmed on location within a 15 to 20 mile radius of Pinewood Studios.

* 2,000,000 plastic daffodils were imported from Japan and used to advertise *Nurse* released in 1959.

* The wardrobe bill for *Carry On Nurse* was £475.

* For his role in *Carry On Sergeant* (1958), Kenneth Williams was paid £800.

* For his role in *Cruising* (1962), Kenneth Williams' pay rose to £5,000 per film; Sid James was the only other team member to earn the same.

* If only four of the films failed, the pass rate would be an astonishing 87.1% – an excellent achievement in anyone's eyes.

* Phil Silvers and Elke Sommer were paid £30,000 each for their roles in *Follow That Camel* (1967) and *Behind* (1975). This was the highest paid in a Carry On.

* *Carry On at your Convenience* (1971) took over five years to get its money back.

* There was a six-week filming schedule for each Carry On film.

* Over eight million viewers watched *Carry On Christmas* in 1969.

* *Carry On Emmannuelle* (1978) was the only film to use two studios - of course Pinewood, the other being Wembley.

* Norman Hudis wrote the first six Carry On films and *Carry On Regardless* (1960) was the least favourite of the films he had written.

* Talbot Rothwell took over as scriptwriter in 1963 and went on to write twenty Carry On films.

* Two films, *Carry On Don't Lose Your Head* (1966) and *Carry On Follow That Camel* (1967) were released without the Carry On prefix. Later they added the Carry On name and as a result they were an instant success.

* On only one occasion did the team venture out of England to shoot a Carry On film and that was to Snowdonia, North Wales, for *Carry On Up the Khyber* in 1968.

* In 1959 *Carry On Nurse* was first in the box office ratings, and it remains a cult film in the USA to this day.

* Bernard Bresslaw's phrase "I Only Arsked" was written into all of the fourteen films he appeared in.

* Charles Hawtrey's first line was usually "Ohh Hello".

* The first Carry On film to be filmed in colour was *Carry On Cruising* in 1962.

* To date there have been fifty-five continuity errors or mistakes made in eighteen of the films, spotted by eagle-eyed Carry On fans.

* Eight Carry On films were never made – *What a Carry On* (1961), *Smoking* (1961), *Flying* (1962), *Spaceman* (1962), *Again Nurse* (1979), *Dallas* (1987), *Down Under* (1988) and *Nursing* (1988).

* To film a Carry On, they usually only used one camera, a Mitchell 35mm. They very rarely used two.

* When released in the USA, *Carry On Nurse* ran for over two and a half years in Los Angeles, California.

* Car Park Number One at Pinewood was used for the taxi yard in *Carry On Cabby* (1963).

* The *Carry On Laughing* compilation television series took over nine months to put together. Gerald Thomas used to view miles and miles of film before editing.

* A £500,000 budget was set aside for *Carry On Down Under* in 1988. Gerald Thomas went to Australia to view possible locations but the film was never made. In one way that was good, as it kept the films totally British.

* All of the main Carry On actors were offered a percentage of the box office takings by Peter Rogers, but they all turned it down and stuck with their one-off payment per film - a big mistake. Only Kenneth Williams admitted this. The offer was made in the early sixties.

* *Carry On Again Nurse* film script written by Norman Hudis had 148 scenes; it was to be the 30th anniversary film, but it was never made.

* *Carry On Sergeant* (1958) made its money back within two weeks of opening in London.

* The first draft script for *Carry On Sergeant* had a total of 180 pages.

* On the back of the success of the first six Carry On films, *Carry On Admiral* by Val Guest was re-released. It only took £11,000 at the box office nationwide, so the people knew what a real Carry On was.

* Every seven years the Carry On films gain a new audience of fans.

* Not one foot of Carry On film was cut or edited without the permission of producer Peter Rogers.

* Jack Douglas was given twelve bottles of champagne from Peter Rogers and Gerald Thomas to welcome him to the Carry On team in 1971.

* The warehouse scene in *Carry On Spying* (1964) was shot at 3 am; probably the earliest start on any film, as 8 am was the norm.

* Filming was usually Monday to Friday on the Carry On films.

* The Carry On television Christmas specials – Barbara Windsor was the only Carry On regular to appear in all four.

* 110 different locations were used in the making of the Carry On films.

* The longest time spent away on location was three weeks to Camber Sands, Rye, Sussex to film *Carry On Follow That Camel* in 1967.

* Talbot Rothwell took just two weeks to write the script for *Carry On Cabby* (1963).

* In the mid-'90s, two Carry On films were put into the top ten films ever made in Britain – *Carry On Cleo* (1964) and *Carry On Up the Khyber* (1968). Both ranked in at equal number ten.

* It took three days to film the dinner party scene at the end of *Carry On Up the Khyber* (1968).

* When Jacki Piper started filming her first film, *Carry On Up The Jungle* (1969), she was offered a contract for the next two years. She went on to appear in four films.

* Jim Dale suggested that he did his own stunts in the Carry On films. Gerald Thomas always used to leave the stunts until the end of filming. Jim actually broke a bone in his arm when he did the stunts in *Carry On Again Doctor* (1969).

* Leslie Phillips got credited for his role in *Carry On Regardless* in 1960 – but the thing was he was never in the film. The credit appeared in a Bristol newspaper.

* The first three Carry On films had a budget of between £70,000 and £80,000.

* In *Carry On Cowboy* (1965) Bernard Bresslaw had to climb fifty feet up into a tree for the shooting scenes.

* *Carry On Sergeant* (1958) was third in the box office ratings.

* Only six of the Carry On films were released on audio cassette: *Don't Lose Your Head* (1966), *Follow That Camel* (1967), *Doctor* (1967), *Up the Khyber* (1968), *Camping* (1969) and *Up the Jungle* (1969).

* One of the production crew used a .22 rifle to shoot the bottle out of Sid James' hand in the 'dinner party scene' in *Carry On Up the Khyber* (1968).

* It was Kenneth Williams who recommended Jim Dale to join the Carry On team. An excellent recommendation as Jim fitted in really well.

* Talbot Rothwell was paid £4,000 for his script of *Carry On Cleo* in 1964.

* Four policemen were used to protect Robin Askwith and Margaret Nolan's scene together on Brighton beach.

* Two policemen and one night watchman were used to guard the fort at Camber Sands.

* The Carry On films finished filming on 27th May 1992 with *Carry On Columbus*.

Left: The South Gates at Pinewood Studios. Scene used in Carry On Screaming (1966)

Right: The Hall of Fame - entering into the Archive Department at Pinewood Studios. It was used as the opening scene in Carry On Spying (1964)

Left: The shops used as the butchers in Carry On Behind (1975). They are situated in Farnham Common, Buckinghamshire

CARRY ON FILM STATISTICS

Totals

31 films were made between
1958 and 1992

Around £6,500,000
was budgeted for the making
of all 31 films

It took 1,303 days = 184.14
weeks = 3.58 years to make
all of the films

Approximately 569.5 miles were
travelled on location (as the crow flies)

Around 1,156 stars and co-stars
appeared in the credits to all 31 films

2,771 minutes of film running time

250,336 feet of film were used

Some 300 reels of film were used

Filmed in colour	23	74%
Filmed in B/W	7	23%
Filmed in colour & B/W	1	3%
Cert A's	22	71%
Cert U's	7	23%
Cert AA	1	3%
Cert PG	1	3%

Averages

1.48 films per year, over a
21-year period, allowing for the
break between 1978 and 1992

£230,000 to produce each
film (approx)

It took six weeks to produce
a film

18.3 miles travelled for each
film on location

37 stars and co-stars per film

89 minutes 39 seconds per film

8,075 feet per film

10 reels per film

SEASONS OF FUN

A common favourite to most, including the Carry On producer Peter Rogers, was, and still is, *Carry On Up the Khyber* (1968).

This is one of the seven films that started its production in April. Meaning that almost a quarter of the thirty-one films produced also saw April as their starting time, the reason obviously being the new financial year which brought windfalls of money and of course laughter. The month of March also equalled April with the start of seven productions, the reason probably being that there must have been some money left in the pot. No films started production in the months of June, August and December, this being due to summer shows and Christmas pantomimes. Of course this resulted in most of the ever-popular Carry On team being "inn it again", as Sid said.

The very first film produced, *Carry On Sergeant* (1958), finished its filming in May, and another nine films followed suit, so a third of the Carry On film series finished their filming within this month.

It took an average of four months for a Carry On film to be released, many during the autumn and winter infact, nineteen of the amazing thirty-one Carry On films (61.3%), brought us, the public, so much cheer and warmed our cockles on these cold long days.

"Cor!"

CARRY ON MEMORY ...
"My Carry On memory is *Carry On Abroad* when I was in bed waiting for Ken Connor to leap on top of me knowing that we and the bed were about to crash through the floor below. Luckily it worked the first time but it was a somewhat nervous moment for Ken and me."
- *June Whitfield CBE*

CARRY ON FILMS
MONTH PRODUCTION STARTED

1.	**March** (*Sergeant, Teacher, Cabby, Again Doctor,* *At Your Convenience, Dick, Behind*)	7	22.6%
	April (*Up The Khyber, Loving, Abroad, Girls,* *That's Carry On, Emmannuelle, Columbus*)	7	22.6%
2.	**October** (*Camping, Up the Jungle,* *Henry, Matron*)	4	12.9%
3.	**September** (*Jack, Don't Lose Your Head,* *Doctor*)	3	9.6%
	November (*Nurse, Constable, Regardless*)	3	9.6%
4.	**January** (*Cruising, Screaming*)	2	6.5%
	May (*Follow That Camel, England*)	2	6.5%
	July (*Cleo, Cowboy*)	2	6.5%
5.	**February** (*Spying*)	1	3.2%
6.	**June, August, December**	0	0%

Spring	16	51.6%
Summer	2	6.5%
Autumn	10	32.3%
Winter	3	9.6%

CARRY ON FILMS
MONTH PRODUCTION FINISHED

1.	**May**	10	32.2%
	(*Sergeant, Cabby, Up the Khyber, Again Doctor, Loving, At Your Convenience, Abroad, Girls, Emmannuelle, Columbus*)		
2.	**April**	4	12.9%
	(*Teacher, Dick, Behind, That's Carry On*)		
	November	4	12.9%
	(*Camping, Up the Jungle, Henry, Matron*)		
3.	**October**	3	9.7%
	(*Jack, Don't Lose Your Head, Doctor*)		
4.	**February**	2	6.5%
	(*Cruising, Screaming*)		
	June	2	6.5%
	(*Follow That Camel, England*)		
	December	2	6.5%
	(*Nurse, Constable*)		
5.	**January**	1	3.2%
	(*Regardless*)		
	March	1	3.2%
	(*Spying*)		
	August	1	3.2%
	(*Cleo*)		
	September	1	3.2%
	(*Cowboy*)		
6.	**July**	0	0%

Spring	15	48.4%
Summer	3	9.7%
Autumn	8	25.8%
Winter	5	16.1%

CARRY ON FILMS
MONTH FILM RELEASED

1.	**November** (*Jack, Cleo, Cowboy, Girls, Emmannuelle*)	5	16.1%
	December (*Don't Lose Your Head, Doctor, At Your Convenience, Abroad, Behind*)	5	16.1%
2.	**February** (*Constable, Camping, Henry, That's Carry On*)	4	12.9%
	August (*Sergeant, Teacher, Screaming, Again Doctor*)	4	12.9%
3.	**March** (*Nurse, Regardless, Up the Jungle*)	3	9.7%
	September (*Follow That Camel, Up the Khyber, Loving*)	3	9.7%
4.	**June** (*Cabby, Spying*)	2	6.5%
	October (*England, Columbus*)	2	6.5%
5.	**April** (*Cruising*)	1	3.2%
	May (*Matron*)	1	3.2%
	July (*Dick*)	1	3.2%
6.	**January**	0	0%

Spring	5	16.1%
Summer	7	22.6%
Autumn	10	32.3%
Winter	9	29.0%

CARRY ON FILMS
LONGEST FILM TO BE RELEASED

Name of film	Finished filming	Film released	Months taken
That's Carry On	April 1977	February 1978	10
Behind	April 1975	December 1975	8
At Your Convenience	May 1971	December 1971	7
Abroad	May 1972	December 1972	7
Screaming	February 1966	August 1966	6
Matron	November 1971	May 1972	6
Girls	May 1973	November 1973	6
Emmannuelle	May 1978	November 1978	6
Columbus	May 1992	October 1992	5
Teacher	April 1959	August 1959	4
Up the Khyber	May 1968	September 1968	4
Up the Jungle	November 1969	March 1970	4
Loving	May 1970	September 1970	4
England	June 1976	October 1976	4
Sergeant	May 1958	August 1958	3
Nurse	December 1958	March 1959	3
Spying	March 1964	June 1964	3
Cleo	August 1964	November 1964	3
Follow That Camel	June 1967	September 1967	3
Camping	November 1968	February 1969	3
Again Doctor	May 1969	August 1969	3
Henry	November 1970	February 1971	3
Dick	April 1974	July 1974	3
Constable	December 1959	February 1960	2
Regardless	January 1961	March 1961	2
Cruising	February 1962	April 1962	2
Cowboy	September 1965	November 1965	2
Don't Lose Your Head	October 1966	December 1966	2
Doctor	October 1967	December 1967	2
Cabby	May 1963	June 1963	1
Jack	October 1963	November 1963	1

CARRY ON PHOTOGRAPHY

	Film	Start date	Finish date	Days
1.	Jack	2.9.63	26.10.63	54
	Cowboy	12.7.65	3.9.65	54
	Follow that Camel	1.5.67	23.6.67	54
	Up The Khyber	8.4.68	31.5.68	54
2.	Regardless	28.11.60	17.1.61	51
3.	Matron	11.10.71	26.11.71	48
4.	Cleo	13.7.64	28.8.64	47
	Screaming	10.1.66	25.2.66	47
	Camping	7.10.68	22.11.68	47
	Henry	12.10.70	27.11.70	47
5.	Don't Lose Your Head	12.9.66	28.10.66	46
	Again Doctor	17.3.69	2.5.69	46
6.	At Your Convenience	22.3.71	7.5.71	45
7.	Cabby	25.3.63	7.5.63	43
8.	Doctor	11.9.67	20.10.67	41
9.	Sergeant	24.3.58	2.5.58	40
	Nurse	3.11.58	12.12.58	40
	Teacher	15.3.59	24.4.59	40
	Constable	9.11.59	18.12.59	40
	Cruising	8.1.62	16.2.62	40
	Up the Jungle	13.10.69	21.11.69	40
	Loving	6.4.70	15.5.70	40
	Abroad	17.4.72	26.5.72	40
	Girls	16.4.73	25.5.73	40
	Behind	10.3.75	18.4.75	40
10.	Dick	4.3.74	11.4.74	39
11.	Columbus	21.4.92	27.5.92	37
12.	Emmannuelle	10.4.78	15.5.78	36
13.	Spying	8.2.64	13.3.64	34
14.	England	3.5.76	4.6.76	33
15.	That's Carry On	18.4.77	20.4.77	3

LONGEST CARRY ON FILM TO MAKE

How long did it take to film a Carry On?

		Weeks	Days
1.	*Jack* (1963)	8	2
2.	*Follow That Camel* (1967)	7	4
	Up the Khyber (1968)	7	4
3.	*Cowboy* (1965)	7	3
4.	*Regardless* (1960)	6	6
5.	*Cleo* (1964)	6	4
	Screaming (1966)	6	4
	Don't Lose Your Head (1966)	6	4
	Camping (1968)	6	4
	Again Doctor (1967)	6	4
	Henry (1970)	6	4
	Matron (1971)	6	4
6.	*That's Carry On* (1977)	6	2
7.	*Cabby* (1963)	6	1
8.	*Constable* (1959)	5	6
	At Your Convenience (1971)	5	6
9.	*Doctor* (1967)	5	5
10.	*Sergeant* (1958)	5	4
	Nurse (1958)	5	4
	Teacher (1959)	5	4
	Cruising (1962)	5	4
	Loving (1970)	5	4
	Abroad (19720	5	4
	Girls (1973)	5	4
	Behind (1975)	5	4
11.	*Up the Jungle* (1969)	5	3
	Dick (1974)	5	3
12.	*Columbus* (1992)	5	1
13.	*Emmannuelle* (1978)	5	0
14.	*Spying* (1964)	4	5
15.	*England* (1976)	4	4

LONGEST RUNNING CARRY ON FILM

Listed below are the running times of the Carry On films and the length of the film used after they were edited. Each film reel contained 1,000 feet of film

		Running time	Length in feet
1.	*Screaming* (1966)	97	8,658
2.	*Follow That Camel* (1967)	95	8,550
	That's Carry On (1977)	95	8,524
	Cowboy (1965)	95	8,499
3.	*Doctor* (1967)	94	8,432
4.	*Cleo* (1964)	92	8,247
5.	*Cabby* (1963)	91	8,230
	Dick (1974)	91	8,201
	Columbus (1992)	91	8,176
	Jack (1963)	91	8,174
6.	*Don't Lose Your Head* (1966)	90	8,150
	Behind (1975)	90	8,139
	Regardless (1960)	90	8,124
	At Your Convenience (1971)	90	8,100
7.	*Henry* (1970)	89	8,046
	Again Doctor (1969)	89	8,010
	Up the Jungle (1969)	89	8,010
	Cruising (1962)	89	8,009
	England (1976)	89	8,000
8.	*Loving* (1970)	88	7,930
	Abroad (1972)	88	7,928
	Girls (1973)	88	7,921
	Camping (1968)	88	7,920
	Emmannuelle (1978)	88	7,916
	Up the Khyber (1968)	88	7,903
9.	*Matron* (1971)	87	7,871
	Spying (1964)	87	7,840
10.	*Constable* (1959)	86	7,781
	Nurse (1958)	86	7,771
	Teacher (1959)	86	7,771
11.	*Sergeant* (1958)	83	7,505

LONGEST DISTANCE

Listed below is the order in which the Carry On team travelled on location.
Mileage calculated approximately as the crow flies

		Location	Miles
1.	Up the Khyber	Snowdonia, North Wales	166
2.	Follow That Camel	Camber Sands, Rye, Sussex	70
3.	At Your Convenience	Brighton, Sussex	60
	Girls	Brighton, Sussex	60
4.	Don't Lose Your Head	Waddesdon Manor, Bucks	28
5.	Jack	Frensham Ponds, Surrey	27
	Columbus	Frensham Ponds, Surrey	27
6.	Sergeant	Stoughton Guildford, Surrey	19
7.	Emmannuelle	Wembley, North London	12
8.	Matron	Ascot, Berkshire	11
9.	Teacher	Ealing, West London	9.5
	Constable	Ealing, West London	9.5
10.	Doctor	Maidenhead Town Hall, Berks	9
	Again Doctor	Maidenhead Town Hall, Berks	9
	Behind	Maidenhead Town Hall, Berks	9
11.	Camping	Northolt, Middlesex	8
12.	Regardless	Park Street, Windsor, Berks	7
	Cabby	Arthur Road, Windsor, Berks	7
	Screaming	Arthur Road, Windsor, Berks	7
	Loving	Arthur Road, Windsor, Berks	7
	Henry	Long Walk, Windsor Castle, Berks	7
13.	Abroad	Slough High Street, Berks	3
14.	Cowboy	Black Park Fulmer, Bucks	2.5
15.	Dick	St Mary's Church, Taplow, Bucks	2
16.	Nurse	Iver Heath, Bucks	1
17.	Cruising	Pinewood Studios (in grounds)	
	Spying	Pinewood Studios (in grounds)	
	Cleo	Pinewood Studios (in grounds)	
	Up the Jungle	Pinewood Studios (in grounds)	
	England	Pinewood Studios (in grounds)	
	That's Carry On	Pinewood Studios (in grounds)	

CARRY ON CASTING

Below is a list of the number of people that appeared in each Carry On film

	Film	Male	Female	Total
1.	*That's Carry On* (1977)	46	28	74
2.	*Regardless* (1960)	40	17	57
3.	*Columbus* (1992)	43	8	51
4.	*Sergeant* (1958)	45	5	50
5.	*Cowboy* (1965)	27	21	48
6.	*Nurse* (1958)	25	20	45
	Loving (1970)	27	18	45
	Emmannuelle (1978)	33	12	45
7.	*Up the Khyber* (1968)	21	21	42
	Behind (1975)	21	21	42
8.	*Cleo* (1964)	22	18	40
	Again Doctor (1969)	18	22	40
9.	*Follow That Camel* (1967)	23	15	38
	Doctor (1967)	21	17	38
10.	*Girls* (1973)	16	21	37
11.	*Constable* (1959)	21	15	36
	Spying (1964)	19	17	36
12.	*Camping* (1968)	14	20	34
	Henry (1970)	25	9	34
13.	*Matron* (1971)	14	19	33
	England (1976)	21	12	33
14.	*Dick* (1974)	21	11	32
15.	*Cabby* (1963)	19	12	31
	Don't Lose Your Head (1966)	16	15	31
16.	*Jack* (1963)	19	10	29
17.	*At Your Convenience* (1971)	16	11	27
18.	*Abroad* (1972)	16	10	26
19.	*Up the Jungle* (1969)	14	9	23
20.	*Cruising* (1962)	17	5	22
21.	*Screaming* (1966)	15	5	20
22.	*Teacher* (1959)	12	6	18

ON LOCATION (FILMS)

After the film script was submitted and read, the location recce accompanied by the production manager and cameraman would seek out possible locations to use in the Carry On films. Once found, a report would be filed to Peter Rogers, the producer, who would decide if they were suitable for filming the external scene.

Most of the external location filming took place within a fifteen-mile radius of Pinewood Studios. For instance Black Park in Fulmer, a stone's throw from the studios, was used in five different films. Locations such as Windsor and Maidenhead were used in no less than eleven of the films – over a third of the series. The furthest travelled on location by the team was to Snowdonia in North Wales, approximately 166 miles as the crow flies from Pinewood. The longest time spent on any location was twenty-one days, which was to Camber Sands, Rye, Sussex. Both of these were in the years 1967/68. There were some sixty-eight journeys to external locations throughout the thirty-one films produced.

Of course all of the internal shots for the films were produced on the sound stages and in the back lot at Pinewood Studios.

The following pages include a comprehensive guide to all of the locations used in the making of the Carry On films.

The Rhododendron Walk (facing south) – Pinewood Studio Gardens.
The scene was used in Carry On Henry (1970), released in 1971

Left: Park Street in Windsor, scene used in Carry On Regardless (1960), Again Doctor (1969) and Loving (1970)

Right: Courts Shop in Maidenhead, scene used in Carry On Camping (1968). The store closed its doors in 2000

Left: Maidenhead Town Hall, scene used in Carry On Doctor (1967), Again Doctor (1969) and Behind (1975). The town hall has now closed down.

LEAGUE OF LOCATIONS USED IN THE FILMS

	Film	Number of times	% of times used
1.	*Camping* (1968)	8	8.1%
	Dick (1974)	8	8.1%
2.	*Constable* (1959)	7	7.1%
	Girls (1973)	7	7.1%
3.	*Loving* (1970)	6	6.1%
	Behind (1975)	6	6.1%
	Cabby (1963)	6	6.1%
	Emmannuelle (1978)	6	6.1%
4.	*At Your Convenience* (1971)	5	5.1%
	Don't Lose Your Head (1966)	5	5.1%
5.	*Regardless* (1960)	4	4.0%
	Again Doctor (1969)	4	4.0%
	Abroad (1972)	4	4.0%
	Follow that Camel (1967)	4	4.0%
6.	*Sergeant* (1958)	3	3.0%
	Screaming (1966)	3	3.0%
	Henry (1970)	3	3.0%
	Matron (1971)	3	3.0%
7.	*Nurse* (1958)	2	2.0%
	Spying (1964)	2	2.0%
	Cowboy (1965)	2	2.0%
	Up the Jungle (1970)	2	2.0%
	England (1976)	2	2.0%
	Doctor (1967)	2	2.0%
8.	*Teacher* (1959)	1	1.0%
	Cruising (1962)	1	1.0%
	Jack (1963)	1	1.0%
	Cleo (1964)	1	1.0%
	Up The Khyber (1968)	1	1.0%
	That's Carry On (1977)	1	1.0%
	Columbus (1992)	1	1.0%

LOCATION GUIDE

Sergeant (1958)
Church in opening wedding scene
Heathercrest National Service Depot

Closing scene as lorry leaves depot

Locations used = 3
Harefield Middlesex
Queens Barracks, Stoughton,
Guildford, Surrey
Rear entrance to Pinewood

Nurse (1958)
Ambulance travelling in opening scene
Haven Hospital

Locations used = 2
Streets of Iver Heath, Bucks
Rear of Pinewood Mansion

Teacher (1959)
Maudlin Street School

Locations used = 1
Drayton Secondary School,
Ealing, West London

Constable (1959)
Opening shot of Police Station
Street shots & town centre
Police on the march
Department store
Post office with K Williams & V Maddern
Church scene
Neglected house

Location used = 7
Hanwell, West London
Ealing, West London
Pinewood Green Estate
F H Rowse, Ealing, West London
Manor Rd, Ealing, West London
Hanwell, West London
St Stephens Road, Ealing

Regardless (1960)
Helping Hands agency
K Williams collecting Yoki
K Williams walking away from taxi
Railway Station

Locations used = 4
Park Street, Windsor, Berks
11 Clarence Road, Windsor
Thames St into Windsor Park
Winsor & Eton Railway Station

Cruising (1962)
Opening shots of cruise liner

Locations used = 1
Southampton Dock, Hants

Cabby (1963)
Opening scenes of Sid James driving
Cab driving scenes

Locations used = 6
Sheet Street, Windsor, Berks
Pinewood Green Estate

Sid James & Jim Dale scene	Black Park Rd, Fulmer, Bucks
Street shots	Windsor, Berks
End chase scenes	Arthur Rd, Windsor, Berks
Hattie orders Cortinas	Bath Road, Taplow, Bucks

Jack (1963)
Spanish coastline

Locations used = 1
Frensham Ponds, Surrey

Spying (1964)
Opening scene of milk float
Victor Maddern walking to lab

Locations used = 2
Rear entrance to Pinewood
Hall of Fame and into the archive
department, Pinewood

Cleo (1964)
Countryside scenes

Locations used = 1
Iver Heath, Bucks

Cowboy (1965)
Horse & coach and fighting scenes

Locations used = 2
Chobham Common, Surrey
and Black Park, Fulmer, Bucks

Screaming (1966)
Dr Watts' house
Dan Dan toilets
Police Station

Locations used = 3
Fulmer Grange, Fulmer, Bucks
South gates, Pinewood
Windsor, Berks

Don't Lose Your Head (1966)
Countryside scenes
French chateau
Duel scene
Ballroom scenes
Driveway scenes

Locations used = 5
Black Park, Fulmer, Bucks
Waddesdon Manor, Bucks
Gardens at Pinewood
Clandon Park House, Surrey
Cliveden, Bucks

Follow That Camel (1967)
Fort scenes
Square tent scene
Cricket ground
Ponsonby Mansion

Locations used = 4
Camber Sands, Rye, Sussex
Mano Farm, Icklesham, Sussex
Swankleys
Osterley Park House, London

Doctor (1967)
Hospital

Nurses' home exterior

Locations used = 2
Maidenhead Town Hall,
St Ives Rd, Berks
The Royal Lancaster Hotel, London

Up the Khyber (1968)
Khyber Pass

Locations used = 1
Beddgelert, Snowdonia,
North Wales

Camping (1968)
Opening cinema scene
Camping shop scene

The Potters' house
Joan Sims' house
Josh Fiddler's camp site
Campsite entrance

Farmhouse
Coach trip to hostel

Locations used = 8
Gerrards Cross, Bucks
Courts, St Ives High St,
Maidenhead, Berks
Pinewood Green Cul-de-sac
Pinewood Green Estate
Orchard at Pinewood
Juniper Cottages,
Burnham Beeches, Bucks
Glebe Farm, Northolt, Middlesex
A412 Iver Heath to Slough

Again Doctor (1969)
Long Hampton Hospital

Nursing Home
Dr Nookie's consulting rooms
Moore/Nookie clinic

Locations used = 4
Maidenhead Town Hall,
St Ives Rd, Berks
Iver Heath, Bucks
Park Street, Windsor, Berks
Rear of Pinewood Mansion

Up the Jungle (1969)
Prof Tinkle's talk scene
Victorian Street

Locations used = 2
The Village Hall, Fulmer, Bucks
Alma Road, Windsor, Berks

Loving (1970)
Opening bus scene
Shop window scene
Wedded Bliss agency
Mr Snooper's house

Locations used = 6
Co-op roundabout, Slough, Berks
Thames St, Windsor, Berks
12 Park St, Windsor, Berks
45 Gloucester Sq, Windsor

Sid Bliss hails a cab	Windsor & Eton Railway Station
32 Rogerham Mansions	Atherton Court, Eton

Henry (1970) — Locations used = 3

Farm where Henry chases wench to	Datchet, Berks
Horse scene	Long Walk, Windsor Castle
Countryside scenes	Black Park, Fulmer, Bucks

At Your Convenience (1971) — Locations used = 5

Sid & Joan's houses	Pinewood Green Estate
Vic Spanner loses his trousers	Odeon Cinema, Uxbridge
Coach trip to Brighton	A412 Iver Heath to Slough
Hotel shot	The Palace Hotel, Brighton
Pier scenes	Palace Pier, Brighton

Matron (1971) — Locations used = 3

Finisham Maternity Hospital	Heatherwood Hospital, Ascot, Berks
Sid & Gang driving along	Ascot High Street, Berks
Closing church scene	Denham Village, Bucks

Abroad (1972) — Locations used = 4

Wundatours shop	65 High St, Slough, Berks
Elsbels hotel	Car park at Pinewood
Dirt Rd leading to Elsbels	Bagshot, Surrey
Coach trip to Elsbels	A412 Iver Heath to Slough

Girls (1973) — Locations used = 7

Council Hall	Town Hall, Slough, Berks
Platform & train departing station	Marylebone Railway Station, London
Sid & Joan's hotel	Palace Hotel, Brighton
Fire station scene	Fire station, Windsor, Berks
Go-kart scene	Palace Pier, Brighton, Sussex
Sid & Babs on moped	B410 Slough to Datchet Rd
Mayor's house	38 Lansdowne Avenue, Slough

Dick (1974)	**Locations used = 8**
Countryside scenes	Black Park, Fulmer, Iver Heath, Bucks; Maidenhead, Thickett, Berks
Rev Flasher's church	St Mary's Church, Hitcham, Bucks
Rev Flasher's home	Stoke Manor, Stoke Poges, Bucks
Prison	Constables Houses, Stoke Poges, Bucks
Horse chasing scenes	Langley Park, Berks
Horse trough scene	The Jolly Woodman, Littleworth Common, Bucks
Behind (1975)	**Locations used = 6**
University	Maidenhead Town Hall, St Ives Rd, Berks
Butchers shop scene	Farnham Common, Bucks
Bernie & Patsy's house	Pinewood Green cul-de-sac
Countryside scenes	Iver Heath, Bucks
Campsite	Orchard at Pinewood
Ian & Adrienne's	Pinewood Green Estate
England (1976)	**Locations used = 2**
Army HQ	Rear of Pinewood Mansion
Army Barracks	Orchard at Pinewood
Emmannuelle (1978)	**Locations used = 5**
Beryl & Larry's house	Pinewood Green cul-de-sac
Launderette	Bourne End, Bucks
Airport	Heathrow Airport, London
Fantasy scenes	Regents Park Zoo, London
Background scenes	St. Mary's Church, Harefield, Middlesex

***That's Carry On* (1977)**
K Williams & B Windsor

Locations used = 1
Projection room 7,
Pinewood Studios

***Columbus* (1992)**
Sea/coastal shots

Locations used = 1
Frensham Ponds, Surrey

Pinewood Green Estate used in Constable (1959),
Cabby (1963), Camping (1968) and At Your Convenience (1971)

St. Mary's Church in the parish of Hitcham Taplow. The scene was used in Carry On Dick (1974)

KISSING SCENES SEEN IN THE EDITED CARRY ON FILMS

1.	*Emmannuelle* (1978)	19
2.	*Loving* (1970)	16
3.	*Don't Lose Your Head* (1966)	14
4.	*Henry* (1970)	9
	Abroad (1972)	9
5.	*Nurse* (1958)	8
	Cabby (1963)	8
6.	*Cleo* (1964)	7
	Up the Khyber (1968)	7
	At Your Convenience (1971)	7
	Girls (1973)	7
7.	*Teacher* (1959)	6
	Screaming (1966)	6
	Matron (1971)	6
	England (1976)	6
8.	*Jack* (1963)	5
9.	*Constable* (1959)	4
	Regardless (1960)	4
	Cowboy (1965)	4
	Follow That Camel (1967)	4
	Doctor (1967)	4
	Up the Jungle (1969)	4
	Dick (1974)	4
	Behind (1975)	4
	Columbus (1992)	4
10.	*Sergeant* (1958)	3
	Cruising (1962)	3
	Camping (1968)	3
11.	*Again Doctor* (1969)	2
12.	*Spying* (1964)	1

Scene used for the factory in Carry On At Your Convenience (1971). It is situated behind the carpenter's workshops at Pinewood Studios

Black Park Country Park, Fulmer, Bucks - scene used in Carry On Cowboy (1965), Don't Lose Your Head (1966) and Dick (1974)

12 Park Street, Windsor, the house, used for the Wedded Bliss Agency in Loving (1970). Below the railings is the stairway used in Regardless ten years earlier in 1960. Just think, the great Sid James once walked through this door!

ALL DRESSED UP WITH SOMEWHERE TO GO!

Over a span of thirty-four years the Carry On team dressed in costumes on nineteen occasions. Their very first outing in *Carry On Sergeant* (1958) saw them in army uniform (stand by your beds). Some eighteen years and twenty-seven films later they had come full circle and used the military uniform of the army again in *Carry On England* (1976).

One of the most popular costumes used was the nurse's uniform (cor!) This was first seen in *Carry On Nurse* (1959) and went on to be used in three more of the series, *Carry On Doctor* (1967), *Carry On Again Doctor* (1969) and finally *Carry On Matron* (1971). There was to be another film – *Carry On Again Nurse* which was written by Norman Hudis and would have been the 30th anniversary film. It was due to be released in 1988, but never got to the production stage. This would have certainly capped an already brilliant medical era of the Carry Ons.

In 1964 it was reportedly said that some of the set seen in the film *Cleopatra* was sold for a total of £155 to the co-star of five Carry On films, Victor Maddern. He later loaned the very same set to another Pinewood Roman production for the sum of £800, making a profit of £645 in the process!

"What a Carry On!"

CARRY ON MEMORY ...

"My first appearance in a Carry On film was as a cabby in *Carry On Cabby*. At the audition when I was asked if I could drive I said yes, although I'd never been behind the wheel of a car in my life! I got the part but only had a fortnight to learn to drive! Full of nerves on my first day's filming on the Pinewood 'Back Lot' I discovered I had to drive fast towards the camera only turning at the last minute. The look on the cameraman's face as I barely missed hitting him is something I shall remember all my life! Carry On films seem to have endured like the traditional British saucy seaside postcard - full of double entendres delivered by caricatures of instantly recognisable characters."
- *Valerie Van Ost*

THEMES USED IN THE FILMS

Army (*Sergeant, Cleo, Up the Khyber, England*)	4	13.3%
Medical (*Nurse, Doctor, Again Doctor, Matron*)	4	13.3%
Holiday (*Cruising, Camping, Abroad*)	3	10.0%
Agency (*Regardless, Loving*)	2	6.7%
Teaching (*Teacher*)	1	3.3%
Police Force (*Constable*)	1	3.3%
Navy (*Jack*)	1	3.3%
Taxi Driver (*Cabby*)	1	3.3%
Espionage (*Spying*)	1	3.3%
Wild West (*Cowboy*)	1	3.3%
Horror (*Screaming*)	1	3.3%
French Revolution (*Don't Lose Your Head*)	1	3.3%
Foreign Legion (*Follow That Camel*)	1	3.3%
Big Game Hunters (*Up the Jungle*)	1	3.3%
Monarchy (*Henry*)	1	3.3%
Factory (*At Your Convenience*)	1	3.3%
Beauty Contest (*Girls*)	1	3.3%
Highwaymen (*Dick*)	1	3.3%
Archaeologists (*Behind*)	1	3.3%
Diplomats (*Emmannuelle*)	1	3.3%
Discovery (*Columbus*)	1	3.3%
Other	14	46.7%
Historical	9	30.0%
Medical	4	13.3%
Holiday	3	10.0%

CARRY ON COSTUMES

1.	*Sergeant* (1958)	costume	modern
2.	*Nurse* (1958)	costume	modern
3.	*Teacher* (1959)		modern
4.	*Constable* (1959)	costume	modern
5.	*Regardless* (1960)		modern
6.	*Cruising* (1962)	costume	modern
7.	*Cabby* (1963)		modern
8.	*Jack* (1963)	period	
9.	*Spying* (1964)		modern
10.	*Cleo* (1964)	period	
11.	*Cowboy* (1965)	period	
12.	*Screaming* (1966)	period	
13.	*Don't Lose Your Head* (1966)	period	
14.	*Follow That Camel* (1967)	period	
15.	*Doctor* (1967)	costume	modern
16.	*Up the Khyber* (1968)	period	
17.	*Camping* (1968)		modern
18.	*Again Doctor* (1969)	costume	modern
19.	*Up the Jungle* (1969)	costume	modern
20.	*Loving* (1970)		modern
21.	*Henry* (1970)	period	
22.	*At Your Convenience* (1971)		modern
23.	*Matron* (1971)	costume	modern
24.	*Abroad* (1972)		modern
25.	*Girls* (1973)		modern
26.	*Dick* (1974)	period	
27.	*Behind* (1975)		modern
28.	*England* (1976)	costume	
29.	*That's Carry On* (1977)	mixture	
30.	*Emmannuelle* (1978)		modern
31.	*Columbus* (1992)	period	

CARRY ON WARDROBE

The wardrobe used in the Carry On films

Wardrobe	Number	Percentage
Modern	11	35.5%
Period costume	10	32.3%
Costume/modern	8	25.8%
Costume	1	3.2%
Mixture	1	3.2%
	31	100%

The pathway leading to the gardens at Pinewood where scenes from Don't Lose Your Head (1966), Follow That Camel (1967), Up the Khyber (1968) and Henry (1970) were filmed

HAVE YOU BEEN REGISTERED?

PEG 1 is probably the number plate that mostly springs to mind from any of the Carry On films. It was one of nineteen used in *Carry On Cabby* in 1963, and was the crowning glory of Charlie Hawkins' Speedee Cab Company.

Obviously *Cabby* saw over a quarter of the vehicles used in the films. Ten of the films never used any registered vehicles, these of course being the historical ones, and those based in foreign places.

It makes you wonder if any of the vehicles seen in the films are still in use today or in someone's private collection somewhere. I expect that a registration collector somewhere holds a number plate used in one of the Carry On films.

Back in 1994 one of the original London taxis (VLX 242) made it to Pinewood Studios and was photographed there, and later popped up on the inside back cover sleeve for a Carry On book – so they are still out there somewhere!

Look at the listed guide to those vehicles used in the films, and see if you know of the whereabouts of any!

CARRY ON MEMORY ...
"I played a very, very minor character in two of the films.
Carry On Sergeant saw me as a glorified extra - part of the platoon.
I went straight into the army after that - National Service! Funnily enough the person this Walworth working-class boy got on really well with was James Villiers, also another glorified extra at this time.
My first film straight OUT of the army was *Carry On Cabby* I think I mouthed one line, 'You bastard', and got to drive an FX2 taxi!
My stepfather was the late Freddie Mills who also featured in two Carry On films, *Constable* and *Regardless*."
- *Don McCorkindale*

CARRY ON VEHICLES

Vehicle registrations seen in the films

1.	Cabby	19	25.3%
2.	Constable	7	9.3%
3.	Loving	6	8.0%
4.	Camping	5	6.7%
	At Your Convenience	5	6.7%
	Matron	5	6.7%
5.	Sergeant	4	5.3%
	Behind	4	5.3%
6.	Screaming	3	4.0%
	Again Doctor	3	4.0%
	Girls	3	4.0%
7.	Regardless	2	2.7%
	England	2	2.7%
	Emmannuelle	2	2.7%
8.	Nurse	1	1.3%
	Teacher	1	1.3%
	Spying	1	1.3%
	Doctor	1	1.3%
	Abroad	1	1.3%

Total of 75 vehicles seen in 19 films *(overall average: almost 4 vehicles per film)*

Pinewood Road, used in Carry On Nurse where the ambulance 705 CPP was driven down in 1958

VEHICLE REGISTRATION PLATES

Used in the Carry On films

Sergeant (1958) = total of 4 seen in the film

R7234660	Army lorry
XMY 636	Old-style sports car
81 BP 39	Army lorry
EMV 675	Laundry van

Nurse (1958) = total of 1 seen in the film

705 CPP	Ambulance

Teacher (1959) = total of 1 seen in the film

373 THE	Car outside of the school

Constable (1959) = total of 7 seen in film

YDU 212	Triumph sports car
892 FPC	Austin Cambridge police car
UUV 133	Austin Cambridge police car
WLU 545	Wages van
AGT 547	Robber's car
285 BH	Tow truck
JHU 319	Police van (black mariah)

Regardless (1960) = total of 2 seen in film

353 HPP	Rolls Royce (black)
TUW 793	London taxi FX2

Cabby (1963) = total of 19 seen in film

VLA 161	London taxi FX2
UYR 137	London taxi FX2
806 MHU	Lambretta scooter
MOW 872	London taxi FX2
MCJ 173	London taxi FX2
PEG 1	Old-style London taxi
WYL 607	London taxi FX2
OWC 167	Ford Cortina Mk1

DILYS LAYE

Dilys first appeared in Carry On Cruising in 1962, she appeared in a total of four films ending with her playing Anthea Meeks in Camping in 1968 where she almost made a mess in Sid's Ford Zephur (725 PHD). These days Dilys is well known for her work in theatre and television.

SGK 473	London taxi FX2
OWC 166	Ford Cortina Mk1
LXA 477	London taxi FX2
726 MRJ	London taxi FX2
OWC 170	Ford Cortina Mk1
OWC 172	Ford Cortina Mk1
OWC 165	Ford Cortina Mk1
OWC 154	Ford Cortina Mk1
CB 6	Jaguar
TLH 595	London taxi FX2
VLX 242	London taxi FX2

Hanwell Library – location used for the police station in Carry On Constable 1959

Spying (1964) = total of 1 seen in film
235 HLC   Milk float

Screaming (1966) = total of 3 seen in film
HS 25   Police car
X 285   Dr Watts' car
MO 1480   Taxi

Doctor (1967) = total of 1 seen in film
MBF 979   Ambulance

The Jolly Woodman Pub, Littleworth Common, Bucks – location used for the horse trough scenes in Carry On Dick 1974

Camping (1968) = total of 5 seen in film
FYB 352D   Vauxhall Viva van
725 PHD   Ford Zephur Mk1
JJM 737F   Coach
CLY 214E   Mini Moke
GWJ 575B   Taxi

Again Doctor (1969) = total of 3 seen in film
SLW 542   Rolls Royce (black)
VLP 687G   London taxi FX2
WMF 930G   Rolls Royce (white)

The Hut in the grounds of Pinewood Studios – location used in Carry On England 1976

Loving (1970) = total of 6 seen in film
NNC 730H   Austin Mini
BGJ 141B   London taxi FX2
AGU 756G   London taxi FX2

YUC 306H	London taxi FX2
SLF 700F	London taxi FX2
NOY 650E	London taxi FX2

At Your Convenience (1971) = total of 5 seen in film
WXF 584	Sid's car
RON 759G	Ford Capri Mk2
VOP 346J	Triumph sports car
VLK 889G	Ford escort van
ONM 871H	Coach

Matron (1971) = total of 5 seen in film
CBH 159B	Ford Zephur Mk2
100 BYV	Rolls Royce (black)
983 ETT	London taxi FX2
BPP 425K	Ambulance
437 BXA	Ambulance

Pinewood Green cul-de-sac, scene used in Camping, 1968, and Emmannuelle ten years later in 1978

Abroad (1972) = total of 1 seen in film
| M76242 | Coach |

Girls (1973) = total of 3 seen in film
FYC 530J	Van outside the hotel
YSF 557L	Fire engine
RGX 44L	Moped

Behind (1975) = total of 4 seen in film
LMV 365K	Austin 1300
MMU 533G	Jaguar
VMY 488G	Archaeologist's van
XPP 226J	Triumph sports car

The triangle on Pinewood Green Estate. Scene used in Carry On Cabby, 1963

England (1976) = total of 2 seen in film
| M198274 | Army truck |
| 334 PML | Army car |

Emmannuelle (1978) = total of 2 seen in film
| OP 55R | Rolls Royce (black) |
| KLT 144P | Triumph TR6 |

The A412 Slough to Iver Heath Road, where the coach scenes for Camping (1968), At Your Convenience (1971) and Abroad (1972) were filmed

CARRY ON MEMORY ...

"The memory which I thought might be quite funny for you was on the film *Carry On Jack*, when I played Captain Hardy for the opening screen credits. They had very cleverly reproduced the famous picture of the death of Nelson, which they cross-faded from the picture to the living image of it. The script I remember was very, very funny, as Nelson kept saying 'Kiss me, Hardy' and I kept saying 'I don't think I'd bother, Sir, I don't think it would be good for you and they won't like it back at the admiralty' to which Nelson again said, 'Kiss me Hardy', which I regrettably did. At this point he expired and I then said the line 'I told you it would not be good for you, Sir!' and then the film started. This in itself was very funny, but what made it hilarious was that we all had to be absolutely frozen and still at the beginning of the shot, but because we all knew what was going to be said, everybody got the giggles. We eventually had to do it about 16 times, with a very irate director saying, 'Come along now, pull yourselves together, this is serious. We have got to get this shot in.'"
- Anton Rodgers

NAMES USED IN THE FILMS

Over the thirty films produced, excluding the compilation film *That's Carry On* (1977), the name Potter was used five times in four films, making it the most common name used. The name Potter first appeared in *Constable* (1960), scripted for Leslie Phillips who played Tom Potter (there's nothing hotter) – really!

There then came a gap of six years before it cropped up again, this time as the Albert Potter played by the versatile actor Jim Dale in Screaming (1966), the boyfriend of Doris Mann, played by Angela Douglas.

In October 1968 *Camping* saw its production when Terry Scott and Betty Marsden played the campoholics Peter and Harriet Potter (on a bicycle made for two).

The final time the name was used was in *Girls* (1973), where Peter Potter was scripted for the second time, now played by the gentle giant of the team, Bernard Bresslaw, Sid's publicity agent.

Talking of the legend Sid James, he actually used his own Christian name six times, in six films, in six years, starting with *Up the Khyber* (1968) where he played Sir Sidney Ruff-Diamond, through to Sidney Fiddler in *Girls* (1973). In between came Sid Boggle in *Camping* (1968), Sidney Bliss in *Loving* (1970), Sid Plummer in *At Your Convenience* (1971) and Sid Carter in *Matron* (1971), where Hattie Jacques played her last role as matron.

Over a span of thirteen years, the larger than life Hattie played the matron on four occasions, obviously in the medical farces starting way back in 1958 with *Nurse*, again nine years later in *Doctor* (1967), through to *Again Doctor* (1969) and finally in *Matron* (1971).

In an interview at Pinewood Studios on 30th May 1999, Peter Rogers the producer of all the Carry Ons said that no star's name ever appeared above the title Carry On. The Carry On name was the star.

WAGES BILLS FOR THE FILMS

1.	*Sergeant* (1958)	£10,985
2.	*Nurse* (1958)	£8,795
3.	*Teacher* (1959)	£10,160
4.	*Constable* (1959)	£12,525
5.	*Regardless* (1960)	£16,900
6.	*Cruising* (1962)	£17,050
7.	*Cabby* (1963)	£19,785
8.	*Jack* (1963)	£21,400
9.	*Spying* (1964)	£18,300
10.	*Cleo* (1964)	£21,070
11.	*Cowboy* (1965)	£18,425
12.	*Screaming* (1966)	£23,625
13.	*Don't Lose Your Head* (1966)	£21,600
14.	*Follow That Camel* (1967)	£50,350
15.	*Doctor* (1967)	£20,250
16.	*Up the Khyber* (1968)	£23,000
17.	*Camping* (1968)	£28,200
18.	*Again Doctor* (1969)	£23,970
19.	*Up the Jungle* (1969)	£26,700
20.	*Loving* (1970)	£20,900
21.	*Henry* (1970)	£23,700
22.	*At Your Convenience* (1971)	£27,100
23.	*Matron* (1971)	£23,595
24.	*Abroad* (1972)	£27,310
25.	*Girls* (1973)	£21,410
26.	*Dick* (1974)	£26,100
27.	*Behind* (1975)	£50,950
28.	*England* (1976)	£20,225
29.	*Emmannuelle* (1978)	£20,750

In the first twenty years of Carry On films a total of £655,130 was paid in wage bills, an average of £22,590 per film, a mere drop in the ocean of Frensham Ponds in comparison to what the films have grossed to date. *Carry On Follow That Camel* and *Behind* were the two films with the highest wage bills, due to payments of £30,000 each to Phil Silvers and Elke Sommer. The second highest was made to Harry H Corbett, who was paid £12,000 for his lead role in *Carry On Screaming*.

WHAT THE CARRY ON FILMS COST TO MAKE

1.	*Sergeant* (1958)	£74,000*
2.	*Nurse* (1958)	£71,000*
3.	*Teacher* (1959)	£78,000*
4.	*Constable* (1959)	£82,500*
5.	*Regardless* (1960)	£100,000*
6.	*Cruising* (1962)	£140,000*
7.	*Cabby* (1963)	£149,986*
8.	*Jack* (1963)	£152,000*
9.	*Spying* (1964)	£148,000*
10.	*Cleo* (1964)	£194,323*
11.	*Cowboy* (1965)	£195,000*
12.	*Screaming* (1966)	£197,500*
13.	*Don't Lose Your Head* (1966)	£200,000*
14.	*Follow That Camel* (1967)	£288,366*
15.	*Doctor* (1967)	£214,000*
16.	*Up the Khyber* (1968)	£260,000*
17.	*Camping* (1968)	£208,354*
18.	*Again Doctor* (1969)	£219,000*
19.	*Up the Jungle* (1969)	£210,000*
20.	*Loving* (1970)	£215,000*
21.	*Henry* (1970)	£223,000*
22.	*At Your Convenience* (1971)	£220,000*
23.	*Matron* (1971)	£224,995*
24.	*Abroad* (1972)	£225,000*
25.	*Girls* (1973)	£205,962*
26.	*Dick* (1974)	£245,000*
27.	*Behind* (1975)	£217,000*
28.	*England* (1976)	£250,000*
29.	*That's Carry On* (1977)	£30,000*
30.	*Emmannuelle* (1978)	£320,000*
31.	*Columbus* (1992)	£2,500,000*

Denotes an estimated calculation

PUBLICITY FOR THE FILMS

		Lobby cards	Posters	Publicity
1.	Sergeant (1958)	8	6	1
2.	Nurse (1958)	5	5	3
3.	Teacher (1959)	8	5	1
4.	Constable (1959)	7	6	5
5.	Regardless (1960)	2	6	1
6.	Cruising (1962)	8	5	6
7.	Cabby (1963)	10	6	1
8.	Jack (1963)	8	6	1
9.	Spying (1964)	9	7	2
10.	Cleo (1964)	10	10	1
11.	Cowboy (1965)	7	10	10
12.	Screaming (1966)	10	4	5
13.	Don't Lose Your Head (1966)	7	2	1
14.	Follow That Camel (1967)	10	2	1
15.	Doctor (1967)	10	6	1
16.	Up the Khyber (1968)	8	6	2
17.	Camping (1968)	10	9	9
18.	Again Doctor (1969)	8	7	1
19.	Up the Jungle (1969)	3	5	2
20.	Loving (1970)	1	3	1
21.	Henry (1970)	14	4	1
22.	At Your Convenience (1971)	8	3	1
23.	Matron (1971)	8	4	1
24.	Abroad (1972)	6	5	2
25.	Girls (1973)	1	4	4
26.	Dick (1974)	8	2	2
27.	Behind (1975)	8	5	1
28.	England (1976)	8	3	3
29.	That's Carry On (1977)	8	4	1
30.	Emmannuelle (1978)	7	4	1
31.	Columbus (1992)	0	2	4

CHAPTER 2
THE TEAM

WHO DID IT AND WHEN?

The mainstay Carry On team consisted of thirteen regulars. These included Kenneth Connor, Peter Butterworth, Bernard Bresslaw, Jim Dale, Jack Douglas, Terry Scott, Patsy Rowlands and the larger than life Hattie Jacques.

We the viewers saw Kenneth Williams star in twenty-six of the thirty-one films, making him the team member with the most appearances. Charles Hawtrey appeared in the greatest-number films in the fewest number of years – in fact he was seen in twenty-three films in fifteen years and it was reported that he could have appeared in other Carry On films, but constant rivalry over top billing put paid to this. Of course Joan Sims was the lady we all loved after seeing her star in twenty-one consecutive films out of the twenty-four she appeared in. This not only made Joan, the top female film performer but also gave her the rating of most overall appearances throughout the Carry On film, television and stage productions combined. This amounted to a massive thirty-eight in total.

When thinking of the Carry Ons Barbara Windsor (along with a few others) always comes to mind; her ten film performances must have been memorable, as eleven other team members actually made more films.

The most famous name to grace the Carry Ons was the lovable Sid James, who appeared in twenty of the films. His rugged exterior was instantly recognisable to the fans and his name is still well known today, many years after his untimely death.

"Stop Messin' About!"

CARRY ON MEMORY ...

"I only spent one day filming on *Carry On Cleo* and one day on *Up the Khyber*, All I can say is I found Jim Dale absolutely charming and friendly, but Kenneth Williams on *Up the Khyber* totally ignored me all day! I was very young and inexperienced at the time, but it taught me as I became more successful to make sure I was polite and welcoming to the young members of any cast I was in!"
- *Wanda Ventham*

THE CARRY ON TEAM

What were they in?

Bernard Bresslaw: *And in My Lady's Chamber, Abroad, Again Christmas, At Your Convenience, Behind, Camping, Christmas 1969, 1973, Cowboy, Dick, Doctor, Follow That Camel, Girls, London, Loving, Matron, Screaming, Up the Jungle, Up the Khyber, Lamp Posts of the Empire, Short Knight, Long Daze, Under the Round Table, What a Carry On!, Who Needs Kitchener?, Wot a Carry On in Blackpool.*

Peter Butterworth: *And in My Lady's Chamber, Abroad, Again Doctor, The Baron Outlook, Behind, Camping, Christmas 1969, 1972, 1973, Cowboy, Dick, Doctor, Don't Lose Your Head, Emmannuelle, England, Follow That Camel, Girls, Henry, Laughing, London, Loving, Screaming, Up the Khyber, The Case of the Coughing Parrot, The Case of the Screaming Winkles, Lamp Posts of the Empire, The Prisoner of Spenda, Short Knight, Long Daze, The Sobbing Cavalier, Under the Round Table, What a Carry On!*

Kenneth Connor: *And in My Lady's Chamber, Abroad, Again Christmas, The Baron Outlook, Behind, Cabby, Christmas 1972, 1973, Cleo, Constable, Cruising, Dick, Emmannuelle, England, Girls, Henry, Laughing, London, Matron, Nurse, Regardless, Sergeant, Teacher, Up the Jungle, The Case of the Coughing Parrot, The Case of the Screaming Winkles, Lamp Posts of the Empire, The Nine Old Cobblers, Norbert Smith – A Life, One in the Eye for Harold, Orgy and Bess, The Prisoner of Spenda, Short Knight, Long Daze, Under the Round Table, What a Carry On!, Who Needs Kitchener?*

Jim Dale: *Again Doctor, Cabby, Cleo, Columbus, Cowboy, Doctor, Don't Lose Your Head, Follow That Camel, Jack, Screaming, Spying.*

Jack Douglas: *And in My Lady's Chamber, Abroad, Behind, Christmas 1972, 1973, Columbus, Dick, Emmannuelle, England, Girls, Laughing, London, Matron, The Case of the Coughing Parrot, The Case of the Screaming Winkles, Lamp Posts of the Empire, The Nine Old Cobblers, Norbert Smith – A Life, One in the Eye for Harold, Orgy and Bess, The Prisoner of Spenda, Short Knight, Long Daze, The Sobbing Cavalier, Under the Round Table, What a Carry On!, Who Needs Kitchener?*

Charles Hawtrey: *Abroad, Again Christmas, Again Doctor, At Your Convenience, Cabby, Camping, Christmas 1969, Cleo, Constable, Cowboy, Doctor, Don't Lose Your Head, Follow That Camel, Henry, Jack, Loving, Matron, Nurse, Regardless, Screaming, Sergeant, Spying, Teacher, Up the Jungle, Up the Khyber.*

45

Hattie Jacques: *Abroad, Again Doctor, At Your Convenience, Cabby, Camping, Christmas 1969, 1972, Constable, Dick, Doctor, Loving, Matron, Nurse, Regardless, Sergeant, Teacher, Orgy and Bess.*

Sid James: *Abroad, Again Christmas, Again Doctor, At Your Convenience, The Baron Outlook, Cabby, Camping, Christmas 1969, 1973, Cleo, Constable, Cowboy, Cruising, Dick, Doctor, Don't Lose Your Head, Girls, Henry, London, Loving, Matron, Regardless, Sid, Up the Jungle, Up the Khyber, Orgy and Bess, The Prisoner of Spenda, The Sobbing Cavalier, What a Carry On!*

Patsy Rowlands: *Abroad, Again Doctor, At Your Convenience, Behind, Dick, Girls, Henry, Loving, Matron, The Nine Old Cobblers.*

Terry Scott: *Again Christmas, Camping, Christmas 1969, Henry, Loving, Matron, Sergeant, Up the Jungle, Up the Khyber.*

Joan Sims: *And in My Lady's Chamber, Abroad, Again Doctor, At Your Convenience, The Baron Outlook, Behind, Camping, Christmas 1972, 1973, Cleo, Constable, Cowboy, Dick, Doctor, Don't Lose Your Head, Emmannuelle, England, Follow That Camel, Girls, Henry, Loving, Matron, Nurse, Regardless, Screaming, Teacher, Up the Jungle, Up the Khyber, The Case of the Coughing Parrot, The Case of the Screaming Winkles, The Nine Old Cobblers, One in the Eye for Harold, The Prisoner of Spenda, Short Knight, Long Daze, The Sobbing Cavalier, Under the Round Table, Who Needs Kitchener?*

Kenneth Williams: *Abroad, Again Doctor, At Your Convenience, Behind, Camping, Cleo, Constable, Cowboy, Cruising, Dick, Doctor, Don't Lose Your Head, Emmannuelle, Follow That Camel, Henry, Jack, Laughing, Christmas Classics, Loving, Matron, Nurse, Regardless, Screaming, Sergeant, Spying, Teacher, Up the Khyber, That's Carry On.*

Barbara Windsor: *And in My Lady's Chamber, Abroad, Again Christmas, Again Doctor, Barbara, The Baron Outlook, Camping, Christmas 1969, 1972, 1973, Dick, Doctor, Girls, Henry, Laughing, Christmas Classics, London, Matron, Spying, Up Yer Cinders, Lamp Posts of the Empire, The Nine Old Cobblers, Norbert Smith – A Life, Orgy and Bess, The Prisoner of Spenda, The Sobbing Cavalier, That's Carry On, What a Carry On!, Who Needs Kitchener? Wot a Carry On in Blackpool.*

THE STARS AND CO-STARS

First and Last Films

Over a period of thirty-four years and thirty-one films, have you ever wondered what the members of this famous team's first and last films were? Now you know …

Team member	First film	Last film
Charles Hawtrey	*Sergeant* (1958)	*Abroad* (1972)
Kenneth Williams	*Sergeant* (1958)	*Emmannuelle* (1978)
Hattie Jacques	*Sergeant* (1958)	*Dick* (1974)
Kenneth Connor	*Sergeant* (1958)	*Emmannuelle* (1978)
Terry Scott	*Sergeant* (1958)	*Matron* (1971)
Shirley Eaton	*Sergeant* (1958)	*Constable* (1959)
Joan Sims	*Nurse* (1958)	*Emmannuelle* (1978)
Leslie Phillips	*Nurse* (1958)	*Columbus* (1992)
Sid James	*Constable* (1959)	*Dick* (1974)
Joan Hickson	*Constable* (1959)	*Girls* (1973)
Liz Fraser	*Regardless* (1960)	*Behind* (1975)
David Lodge	*Regardless* (1960)	*England* (1976)
Dilys Laye	*Cruising* (1962)	*Camping* (1968)
Jim Dale	*Cabby* (1963)	*Columbus* (1992)
Peter Gilmore	*Cabby* (1963)	*Columbus* (1992)
Bernard Cribbins	*Jack* (1963)	*Columbus* (1992)
Barbara Windsor	*Spying* (1964)	*Dick* (1974)
Hugh Futcher	*Spying* (1964)	*Behind* (1975)
Jon Pertwee	*Cleo* (1964)	*Columbus* (1992)
Bernard Bresslaw	*Cowboy* (1965)	*Behind* (1975)
Peter Butterworth	*Cowboy* (1965)	*Emmannuelle* (1978)
Angela Douglas	*Cowboy* (1965)	*Up the Khyber* (1968)
Julian Holloway	*Follow That Camel* (1967)	*England* (1976)
Valerie Leon	*Up the Khyber* (1968)	*Girls* (1973)
Patsy Rowlands	*Again Doctor* (1969)	*Behind* (1975)
Jacki Piper	*Up the Jungle* (1969)	*Matron* (1971)
Richard O'Callaghan	*Loving* (1970)	*At Your Convenience* (1971)
Jack Douglas	*Matron* (1971)	*Columbus* (1992)

CARRY ON MEMORY ...

"Up until the day I agreed to do the first Carry On I had been a serious stuntman and thought that films such as Carry On were a joke, but I found out that although the money was tight they expected the best. I had some great times making these cut-price movies, made all the better by getting to know some wonderful people like Dora Bryan, Bill Owen, Sid James (who was the best tapper in the business), Joan Sims, whom I used to drop off home on many occasions as it was on my way, and Phil Silvers who on screen was one of my favourites. Not a lot of people know this, but at the time of my first Carry On I had been dabbling in a bit of theatre work in such plays as *Mr Roberts* with Tyrone Power and *Wish You Were Here* and a lot of muscle guys which attended the audition for Carry On, among them Sean Connery, who was a top Mr Universe contestant at the time. It was always a great pleasure to work on the Carry On films, as I knew so many of the stars personally. Alas so many have gone on to the big heavenly stage and I bet they keep 'em laughing there too. I can honestly say that whenever I was called on to a Carry On film set I knew that I was going to work and I was going to enjoy myself."
- *Nosher Powell*

The Gardens of Fragrance where Kenneth Williams and Sid James fought their duel in Carry On Don't Lose Your Head (1966)

CARRY ON MEMORY ...

"I was in the first Carry On film only. I thought the film was dreadful, one of the black and white films of the last century best forgotten. It was rather boring to be in, only lightened at times by Kenneth Williams and his outrageous anecdotes."
- *Gerald Campion*

CARRY ON LEAGUE OF STARS & CO-STARS STARRING IN THE FILMS

		No of films	% of films
1.	Kenneth Williams	26	83.9%
2.	Joan Sims	24	77.4%
3.	Charles Hawtrey	23	74.2%
4.	Sid James	19	61.3%
5.	Kenneth Connor	17	54.8%
6.	Peter Butterworth	16	51.6%
7.	Hattie Jacques	14	45.2%
	Bernard Bresslaw	14	45.2%
8.	Michael Nightingale	13	41.9%
9.	Jim Dale	10	32.3%
	Peter Gilmore	10	32.3%
	Barbara Windsor	10	32.3%
10.	Patsy Rowlands	9	29.0%
	Marianne Stone	9	29.0%
11.	Jack Douglas	8	25.8%
	Julian Holloway	8	25.8%
12.	Terry Scott	7	22.6%
	Cyril Chamberlain	7	22.6%
	Gertan Klaber	7	22.6%
	Frank Forsyth	7	22.6%
	Hugh Futcher	7	22.6%
	Billy Cornelius	7	22.6%
	Lucy Griffiths	7	22.6%
13.	Tom Clegg	6	19.4%
	Sally Douglas	6	19.4%
	Valerie Leon	6	19.4%
	Margaret Nolan	6	19.4%
	Brian Osborne	6	19.4%
	Derek Francis	6	19.4%
	Simon Cain	6	19.4%
14.	Victor Maddern	5	16.1%
	Bill Maynard	5	16.1%
	Alexandra Dane	5	16.1%

PETER GILMORE
Peter, of the Onedian Line fame in the '70s, crops up in a third of all the Carry On films made. He fitted in well with the team and his versatility is shown by his playing a number of different characters.

HUGH FUTCHER
Hugh first appeared in Carry On Spying in 1964. He can be seen lying on his bed of nails in the Kasbah. Hugh went on to star in another six films, his last role being a painter in Carry On Behind (1975). Once seen, his face was never forgotten - especially by Carry On fans.

49

	Joan Hickson	5	16.1%
	David Lodge	5	16.1%
	Norman Mitchell	5	16.1%
	Valerie Shute	5	16.1%
	Michael Ward	5	16.1%
	Anthony Sagar	5	16.1%
	Amelia Bayntun	5	16.1%
15.	Esma Cannon	4	12.9%
	Julian Orchard	4	12.9%
	Leslie Phillips	4	12.9%
	Terence Longdon	4	12.9%
	Jacki Piper	4	12.9%
	Eric Barker	4	12.9%
	Larry Dann	4	12.9%
	Angela Douglas	4	12.9%
	Liz Fraser	4	12.9%
	Dilys Laye	4	12.9%
	Bill Owen	4	12.9%
	Brian Oulton	4	12.9%
	Jon Pertwee	4	12.9%
	June Whitfield	4	12.9%
	Ian Wilson	4	12.9%
	Jeremy Connor	4	12.9%
	Valerie Van Ost	4	12.9%
16.	Bernard Cribbins	3	9.7%
	Shirley Eaton	3	9.7%
	Judith Furse	3	9.7%
	Angela Grant	3	9.7%
	Linda Hooks	3	9.7%
	Renee Houston	3	9.7%
	Harry Locke	3	9.7%
	Brian Rowlinson	3	9.7%
	Norman Rossington	3	9.7%
	Jimmy Thomson	3	9.7%
	Johnny Briggs	3	9.7%
	Ed Devereaux	3	9.7%
	Leon Greene	3	9.7%
	Dominique Don	3	9.7%

LIZ FRASER
Liz starred in four Carry On films. The first was Regardless (1960), and Cruising, Cabby and Behind followed over the next 15 years. Her last Carry On appearance was in the stage show Carry On Laughing (with The Slimming Factory) which ran on the 1975 Scarborough summer season. Jack Douglas, Kenneth Connor and Peter Butterworth also appeared. Liz is an excellent actress who has appeared in many other films and TV productions.

RICHARD O'CALLAGHAN
Richard was a new face brought into the team for Carry On Loving (1970). He starred in two films, working closely with Jacki Piper on both occasions.

SHIRLEY EATON
Shirley starred in three of the early Carry Ons, adding a touch of glamour to the team. She actually ranks at number two behind Charles Hawtrey in the overall ratios, as she made three Carry Ons in two years.

	Vicki Smith	3	9.7%
17.	Frankie Howerd	2	6.5%
	Amanda Barrie	2	6.5%
	Norman Chappell	2	6.5%
	Kenneth Cope	2	6.5%
	Alan Curtis	2	6.5%
	Windsor Davis	2	6.5%
	Fenella Fielding	2	6.5%
	Carol Hawkins	2	6.5%
	Rosalind Knight	2	6.5%
	Jimmy Logan	2	6.5%
	Wendy Richard	2	6.5%
	Elspeth March	2	6.5%
	Betty Marsden	2	6.5%
	Freddie Mills	2	6.5%
	Bill Pertwee	2	6.5%
	Eric Pohlmann	2	6.5%
	Anton Rodgers	2	6.5%
	John Carlin	2	6.5%
	Peter Boita	2	6.5%
	Vincent Ball	2	6.5%
	Patrick Cargill	2	6.5%
	Pat Coombs	2	6.5%
	Sally Geeson	2	6.5%
	Irene Handl	2	6.5%
	Anita Harris	2	6.5%
	Richard O'Callaghan	2	6.5%
	Percy Herbert	2	6.5%
	Peter Jones	2	6.5%
	Noel Dyson	2	6.5%
	Ambrosine Philpotts	2	6.5%
	June Jago	2	6.5%
	Gilly Grant	2	6.5%
	Anna Karen	2	6.5%
	Alan Curtis	2	6.5%
	John Clive	2	6.5%
	Ian Whittaker	2	6.5%
	Hilda Fenemore	2	6.5%

ALEXANDRA DANE
Alexandra was first seen as an instructor in Carry On Doctor (1967), putting Charles Hawtrey through his maternity exercises. She starred in three more films and finally, in 1975, was seen in a low-cut dress in Carry On Behind. Cor!

VALERIE LEON
Tall, beautiful and glamorous. These three words describe this star of six Carry On films. Valerie owned an Austin GT with the number plate VL1 in the early '70s. She is still as beautiful now as when the fans saw her in the films.

FENELLA FIELDING
Fenella starred in two films, Regardless (1960) and Screaming (1966), which was undoubtedly one of the finest performances in the entire series. She is an approachable lady who always has time for her fans.

	David Williams	2	6.5%
	Leigh Madison	2	6.5%
	Laraine Humphreys	2	6.5%
	Philip Stone	2	6.5%
	John Antrobus	2	6.5%
18.	Roy Castle	1	3.2%
	Harry H Corbett	1	3.2%
	Suzanne Danielle	1	3.2%
	William Hartnell	1	3.2%
	Imogen Hassall	1	3.2%
	Sherrie Hewson	1	3.2%
	Wilfred Hyde-White	1	3.2%
	Diane Langton	1	3.2%
	Warren Mitchell	1	3.2%
	Bob Monkhouse	1	3.2%
	Lance Percival	1	3.2%
	Ted Ray	1	3.2%
	Dany Robin	1	3.2%
	Phil Silvers	1	3.2%
	Elke Sommer	1	3.2%
	Penelope Keith	1	3.2%
	Ian Lavender	1	3.2%
	George Layton	1	3.2%
	Kenny Lynch	1	3.2%
	Michael Medwin	1	3.2%
	Juliet Mills	1	3.2%
	Patrick Mower	1	3.2%
	Dandy Nicholls	1	3.2%
	Milo O'Shea	1	3.2%
	Richard O'Sullivan	1	3.2%
	Cecil Parker	1	3.2%
	Nicholas Parsons	1	3.2%
	Beryl Reid	1	3.2%
	Arnold Ridley	1	3.2%
	Cardew Robinson	1	3.2%
	Frank Thornton	1	3.2%
	Dora Bryan	1	3.2%
	Terence Alexander	1	3.2%

FRANK THORNTON
Frank only appeared in one Carry On - Screaming in 1966. He played Mr Jones, manager of the shop the dummy was stolen from. He went on to Captain Peacock fame 'Are You Being Served' and 'Last of the Summer Wine'.

MARC SINDEN
Marc is the son of Sir Donald. He co-starred in Columbus (1992) as Captain Perez. Marc once said he was honoured to have appeared in a Carry On film. He now runs his own production company.

CHRISTINE OZANNE
Christine's only Carry On role was in Nurse, made in 1958 and released in 1959. She can be seen cleaning the hospital in the background on a couple of occasions. She now runs her own Shakespeare touring company.

Robin Askwith	1	3.2%
Wilfred Brambell	1	3.2%
Ray Brooks	1	3.2%
Marc Sinden	1	3.2%
Jeremy Desmonde	1	3.2%
Judy Geeson	1	3.2%
Deryck Guyler	1	3.2%
Sheila Hancock	1	3.2%
Melvyn Hayes	1	3.2%
Patricia Hayes	1	3.2%
Donald Hewlett	1	3.2%
Donald Houston	1	3.2%
Geoffrey Hughes	1	3.2%
Jill Ireland	1	3.2%
Christine Ozanne	1	3.2%
Michael Balfour	1	3.2%
Susan Shaw	1	3.2%
Gerald Campion	1	3.2%
Ronnie Stevens	1	3.2%
Richard O'Brien	1	3.2%
Bob Todd	1	3.2%
Bill Kenwright	1	3.2%
Mike Grady	1	3.2%
Olga Lowe	1	3.2%
Elizabeth Knight	1	3.2%
David Kernan	1	3.2%
Richard Wilson	1	3.2%

JACKI PIPER
Jacki's first film was Up the Jungle in 1969. She was offered a two-year contract which was extended for her to appear in four films, with her final appearance in Matron.

ALAN HUME
Alan, who worked on sixteen Carry On films, is a very kind man and a legend in the film industry.

ANGELA GRANT
Angela's first appearance was in Follow That Camel in 1967. She was also in Up the Khyber in 1968, with her final film being Girls, where she played a beauty contestant - cor!

CARRY ON MEMORY ...

"I was young and foolish. I never did it again! I was paid £25 a day.
The cream fight was fun. The cream was real, so was the stench."
- Mike Grady

SUSTAINED APPEARANCES

in Carry On Films

These are the top ten sustained appearances in the Carry On film series by the stars without missing one. (All statistics compiled from 1958 to 1992.)

1.	Joan Sims	21	67.7%
	from *Cleo* (1964) to *Emmannuelle* (1978)		
2.	Charles Hawtrey	18	58.0%
	from *Cabby* (1963) to *Matron* (1971)		
3.	Sid James	12	38.7%
	Doctor (1967) to *Dick* (1974)		
4.	Kenneth Williams	11	35.5%
	from *Jack* (1963) to *Camping* (1968)		
5.	Jack Douglas	9	29.0%
	from *Matron* (1972) to *Columbus* (1992)		
	Jim Dale	9	29.0%
	from *Cabby* (1963) to *Doctor* (1967)		
6.	Kenneth Connor	8	25.8%
	from *Abroad* (1972) to *Emmannuelle* (1978)		
	Patsy Rowlands	8	25.8%
	from *Loving* (1970) to *Behind* (1975)		
	Peter Butterworth	8	25.8%
	from *Cowboy* (1965) to *Camping* (1968)		
7.	Bernard Bresslaw	6	19.4%
	from *At Your Convenience* (1971) to *Behind* (1975)		
8.	Hattie Jacques	5	16.1%
	from *Sergeant* (1958) to *Regardless* (1960)		
9.	Terry Scott	4	12.9%
	from *Camping* (1968) to *Henry* (1970)		
	Barbara Windsor	4	12.9%
	from *Abroad* (1972) to *Dick* (1974)		
	Esma Cannon	4	12.9%
	from *Constable* (1959) to *Cabby* (1963)		
10.	Leslie Phillips	3	9.7%
	from *Nurse* (1958) to *Constable* (1959)		
	Liz Fraser	3	9.7%
	from *Regardless* (1960) to *Cabby* (1963)		

CARRY ON RATIOS

This list below shows the stars and how many Carry On films they appeared in over a number of years. Figures do not include the That's Carry On (1977) compilation and Columbus (1992).

1.	Charles Hawtrey	23 films in 15 years	65.2%
2.	Shirley Eaton	3 films in 2 years	66.6%
3.	Jim Dale	10 films in 7 years	70.0%
4.	Patsy Rowlands	9 films in 7 years	77.7%
5.	Bernard Bresslaw	14 films in 11 years	78.6%
6.	Joan Sims	24 films in 20 years	83.3%
7.	Kenneth Williams	25 films in 21 years	84.0%
8.	Sid James	19 films in 16 years	84.2%
9.	Peter Butterworth	16 films in 14 years	87.5%
10.	Jack Douglas	7 films in 7 years	100.0%
	Valerie Leon	6 films in 6 years	100.0%
	Angela Douglas	4 films in 4 years	100.0%
	Jacki Piper	4 films in 4 years	100.0%
11.	Hattie Jacques	14 films in 16 years	114.2%
12.	Barbara Windsor	9 films in 11 years	122.2%
13.	Kenneth Connor	17 films in 21 years	123.5%
14.	Julian Holloway	8 films in 10 years	125.0%
15.	Hugh Futcher	7 films in 12 years	171.4%
16.	Dilys Laye	4 films in 7 years	175.0%
17.	Terry Scott	7 films in 15 years	214.2%

29 films made in 21 years 72.4%

IN HOW MANY SCENES THE STARS WERE SEEN IN THE EDITED VERSIONS OF THE FILMS

Sergeant (1958)

Kenneth Connor	38
Charles Hawtrey	24
Kenneth Williams	22
Hattie Jacques	9
Terry Scott	2

Teacher (1959)

Kenneth Williams	38
Kenneth Connor	37
Joan Sims	30
Charles Hawtrey	29
Hattie Jacques	28

Regardless (1960)

Kenneth Connor	36
Kenneth Williams	32
Sid James	31
Charles Hawtrey	23
Joan Sims	22
Hattie Jacques	5

Cabby (1963)

Sid James	59
Hattie Jacques	38
Kenneth Connor	35
Charles Hawtrey	35
Jim Dale	7

Nurse (1958)

Kenneth Connor	30
Kenneth Williams	30
Joan Sims	23
Hattie Jacques	19
Charles Hawtrey	17

Constable (1959)

Sid James	40
Kenneth Connor	36
Kenneth Williams	35
Charles Hawtrey	26
Hattie Jacques	21
Joan Sims	16

Cruising (1962)

Kenneth Connor	49
Kenneth Williams	42
Sid James	41

Jack (1963)

Charles Hawtrey	38
Kenneth Williams	32
Jim Dale	8

Spying (1964)
Kenneth Williams 53
Charles Hawtrey 41
Barbara Windsor 36
Jim Dale 15

Cowboy (1965)
Sid James 46
Jim Dale 33
Kenneth Williams 28
Peter Butterworth 13
Charles Hawtrey 13
Joan Sims 12
Bernard Bresslaw 7

Don't Lose Your Head (1966)
Kenneth Williams 49
Sid James 48
Peter Butterworth 43
Jim Dale 34
Joan Sims 32
Charles Hawtrey 24

Doctor (1967)
Bernard Bresslaw 29
Hattie Jacques 28
Kenneth Williams 27
Jim Dale 26
Sid James 23
Charles Hawtrey 13
Barbara Windsor 12
Peter Butterworth 11
Joan Sims 10

Cleo (1964)
Kenneth Williams 48
Kenneth Connor 40
Sid James 37
Jim Dale 26
Charles Hawtrey 25
Joan Sims 13

Screaming (1966)
Peter Butterworth 36
Jim Dale 35
Kenneth Williams 25
Joan Sims 10
Bernard Bresslaw 9
Charles Hawtrey 5

Follow That Camel (1967)
Jim Dale 32
Kenneth Williams 28
Peter Butterworth 27
Bernard Bresslaw 19
Charles Hawtrey 15
Joan Sims 8

Up the Khyber (1968)
Terry Scott 31
Peter Butterworth 27
Bernard Bresslaw 26
Kenneth Williams 25
Sid James 25
Charles Hawtrey 25
Joan Sims 19

Camping (1968)

Sid James	35
Bernard Bresslaw	35
Kenneth Williams	30
Barbara Windsor	28
Terry Scott	24
Joan Sims	23
Hattie Jacques	22
Charles Hawtrey	16
Peter Butterworth	9

Up the Jungle (1969)

Sid James	47
Kenneth Connor	35
Joan Sims	32
Bernard Bresslaw	23
Terry Scott	22
Charles Hawtrey	9

Henry (1970)

Sid James	65
Kenneth Williams	38
Joan Sims	32
Terry Scott	31
Charles Hawtrey	22
Barbara Windsor	16
Kenneth Connor	14
Peter Butterworth	2
Patsy Rowlands	2

Matron (1971)

Sid James	44
Hattie Jacques	42
Kenneth Williams	29

Again Doctor (1969)

Jim Dale	65
Kenneth Williams	38
Charles Hawtrey	36
Hattie Jacques	28
Sid James	26
Joan Sims	20
Barbara Windsor	16
Patsy Rowlands	12
Peter Butterworth	2

Loving (1970)

Sid James	39
Hattie Jacques	31
Joan Sims	18
Bernard Bresslaw	15
Kenneth Williams	14
Terry Scott	14
Charles Hawtrey	12
Patsy Rowlands	7
Peter Butterworth	1

At Your Convenience (1971)

Sid James	48
Bernard Bresslaw	37
Kenneth Williams	33
Joan Sims	32
Patsy Rowlands	23
Charles Hawtrey	20
Hattie Jacques	11

Abroad (1972)

Sid James	50
Kenneth Williams	40
Peter Butterworth	38

Terry Scott   23
Bernard Bresslaw 22
Kenneth Connor   16
Barbara Windsor   12
Charles Hawtrey   9
Joan Sims   7
Patsy Rowlands   3
Jack Douglas   1

Joan Sims   37
Kenneth Connor   36
Barbara Windsor   32
Charles Hawtrey   28
Bernard Bresslaw 23
Hattie Jacques   13
Jack Douglas   5
Patsy Rowlands   2

Girls (1973)
Sid James   46
Bernard Bresslaw 34
Joan Sims   26
Barbara Windsor   25
Kenneth Connor   22
Peter Butterworth 21
Jack Douglas   19
Patsy Rowlands   14

Dick (1974)
Sid James   58
Kenneth Williams 44
Jack Douglas   42
Barbara Windsor   35
Bernard Bresslaw 30
Peter Butterworth 27
Kenneth Connor   19
Joan Sims   18
Hattie Jacques   16
Patsy Rowlands   1

Behind (1975)
Kenneth Williams 40
Jack Douglas   34
Bernard Bresslaw 28
Kenneth Connor   27
Peter Butterworth 25
Patsy Rowlands   22
Joan Sims   20

England (1976)
Kenneth Connor   63
Jack Douglas   40
Joan Sims   22
Peter Butterworth 12

Emmannuelle (1978)
Jack Douglas   26
Kenneth Williams 18
Kenneth Connor   16
Joan Sims   13
Peter Butterworth 13

Columbus (1992)
Jim Dale   61
Jack Douglas   8

TOTAL NUMBER OF SCENES IN WHICH THE STARS APPEARED IN THE FILMS

Name	Scenes	Average per film
Sid James	808	42.5
Kenneth Connor	589	34.6
Kenneth Williams	838	33.5
Jim Dale	338	30.7
Bernard Bresslaw	337	24.1
Barbara Windsor	212	23.6
Hattie Jacques	311	22.2
Charles Hawtrey	505	21.9
Jack Douglas	175	21.8
Terry Scott	147	21.0
Joan Sims	495	20.6
Peter Butterworth	307	19.2
Patsy Rowlands	86	9.6

Behind every great actor is a great woman - in this case there are two! Val James, widow of Sid James (left), taken at Carry On Screaming, 5th November 2000, and Sid's daughter Sue James (right). Sue was a consultant for the documentary 'The Unforgettable Sid James'. The photo was taken at Carry On Celebrating, 29th April 2001.

BILLING RUNNING ORDERS

Sid James	1,1,1,1,1,1,1,3,1,1,1,2,1,1,1,1,1,1,1.	**22**
Kenneth Williams	8,4,5,5,4,2,1,1,2,2,2,2,4,2,2,2,3,2,2,2,2,2,1,1.	**65**
Charles Hawtrey	7,3,3,4,3,3,4,3,3,4,4,4,5,4,3,4,4,3,3,3,3,3,3.	**83**
Kenneth Connor	6,2,2,3,2,3,4,4,5,7,8,6,4,8,4,1,3.	**72**
Jim Dale	9,7,5,6,3,3,3,2,5,2,1.	**46**
Joan Sims	9,7,7,5,5,5,5,5,5,6,10,5,3,5,4,5,4,5,5,4,3,6,5,10,5.	**133**
Barbara Windsor	2,9,6,6,6,7,9,2,3.	**50**
Bernard Bresslaw	7,8,8,8,6,7,6,6,6,6,8,5,5,3.	**89**
Hattie Jacques	13,5,6,8,11,2,6,8,7,4,4,4,7,4.	**89**
Peter Butterworth	6,7,6,3,7,7,9,9,12,10,5,6,7,8,9,6.	**117**
Terry Scott	33,8,5,7,7,5,9.	**74**
Jack Douglas	26,20,8,9,7,5,4,17.	**96**
Patsy Rowlands	8,11,25,10,13,18,9,10,12.	**116**

The rear of the mansion house at Pinewood Studios.
The scene was used in Carry On Nurse in 1958, released in 1959.

CARRY ON LEAGUE
OF TOP BILLINGS

1.	Sid James	1.2
2.	Kenneth Williams	2.6
3.	Charles Hawtrey	3.6
4.	Kenneth Connor	4.2
	Jim Dale	4.2
5.	Joan Sims	5.5
6.	Barbara Windsor	5.6
7.	Bernard Bresslaw	6.4
	Hattie Jacques	6.4
8.	Peter Butterworth	7.3
9.	Terry Scott	10.6
10.	Jack Douglas	12.0
11.	Patsy Rowlands	12.8

CARRY ON MEMORY ...

"*Carry On London* - It was a great thrill to be on stage live with the team and we had a wonderful time. I worked mostly with Sid James and we were great mates. During rehearsals he said to me, 'Don't ad-lib with me on stage because I can't ad-lib', but he also said 'You will always get my lines the same every night and if there are any ad-libs to be done, you do them'. It was a wonderful relationship, which we both enjoyed. We opened at the Birmingham Hippodrome and then went to the Victoria Palace where we packed for eighteen months."
- *Jack Douglas*

CARRY ON FILMS
THE PEOPLE BEHIND THE SCENES

Have you ever thought about those people whose faces were never seen and how many Carry On films they worked on? Now you know ...

Job description	Name	Number of films	% Worked on
Producer	Peter Rogers	31	100%
Director	Gerald Thomas	31	100%
Screenplay	Talbot Rothwell	21	67.7%
	Norman Hudis	7	22.6%
	Dave Freeman	3	9.6%
	Sid Colin	2	6.5%
	Dave Pursall	1	3.2%
	Jack Seddon	1	3.2%
	Tony Church	1	3.2%
	Lance Peters	1	3.2%
Music	Eric Rogers	23	74.2%
	Bruce Montgomery	6	19.4%
	Douglas Gamley	1	3.2%
	Max Harris	1	3.2%
	John Du Prez	1	3.2%
Director of Photography	Alan Hume	16	51.6%
	Ernest Steward	10	32.3%
	Reginald Wyer	2	6.5%
	Peter Hennessy	1	3.2%
	Ted Scaife	1	3.2%
	Tony Imi	1	3.2%
Camera Operator	Godrey Godar	9	29.0%
	James Balden	9	29.0%
	Alan Hume	4	12.9%
	Jimmy Devis	4	12.9%
	Dudley Lovell	2	6.5%
	Alan Hall	1	3.2%
	Derek Browne	1	3.2%
	Neil Binney	1	3.2%

	Martin Hume	1	3.2%
Art Director	Lionel Couch	11	35.5%
	Alex Vetchinsky	6	19.4%
	Bert Davey	3	9.6%
	Carmen Dillon	2	6.5%
	Jack Stephens	2	6.5%
	Jack Shampan	2	6.5%
	Cedric Dawe	1	3.2%
	John Blezard	1	3.2%
	Robert Jones	1	3.2%
	Peter Childs	1	3.2%
Assistant Director	Jack Causey	7	22.6%
	David Bracknell	6	19.4%
	Peter Bolton	5	16.1%
	Bert Batt	2	6.5%
Production Manager	Jack Swinburne	12	38.7%
	Frank Bevis	9	29.0%
	Roy Goddard	6	19.4%
Editor	Alfred Roome	15	48.4%
	John Shirley	5	16.1%
	Archie Ludski	4	12.9%
	Rod Keys	3	9.6%
	Peter Boita	2	6.5%
Sound/Dubbing/Editor	Chris Lancaster	4	12.9%
	Colin Miller	4	12.9%
	Arthur Rideout	3	9.6%
	Peter Best	3	9.6%
	Patrick Foster	3	9.6%
	Seymour Logie	2	6.5%
	Roger Cherrill	2	6.5%
	Leslie Higgins	2	6.5%
	Wally Nelson	2	6.5%
	Brian Holland	2	6.5%
Make-up	Geoffrey Rodway	23	74.2%
	George Blackler	5	16.1%
	Jim Hydes	2	6.5%

	W T Partleton	1	3.2%
	Sarah Monzani	1	3.2%
	Amanda Knight	1	3.2%
Continuity	Penny Daniels	6	19.4%
	Joy Mercer	4	12.9%
	Marjorie Lavelly	4	12.9%
	Rita Davidson	3	9.6%
	Joan Davies	2	6.5%
	Gladys Goldsmith	2	6.5%
	Josephine Knowles	2	6.5%
	Susannah Merry	1	3.2%
	Doreen Dernley	1	3.2%
	Tilly Day	1	3.2%
	Olga Brook	1	3.2%
	Yvonne Richards	1	3.2%
	Jane Buck	1	3.2%
Casting Director	Betty White	6	19.4%
	John Owen	2	6.5%
	Gina Jay	1	3.2%
Hairdressing	Stella Rivers	21	67.7%
	Biddy Crystal	4	12.9%
	Olga Angelinetta	2	6.5%
	Ann Fordyce	1	3.2%
	Sue Love	1	3.2%
	Sarah Love	1	3.2%
	Pearl Orton	1	3.2%
Costume Designer	Courtenay Elliott	11	35.5%
	Joan Ellacott	5	16.1%
	Yvonne Caffin	4	12.9%
	Emma Selby-Walker	4	12.9%
	Anna Duse	1	3.2%
	Julie Harris	1	3.2%
	Cynthia Tingey	1	3.2%

Audrey Skinner, personal assistant to Peter Rogers. Audrey is one of the main people behind the scenes of the Carry On business.

CARRY ON SCRIPTWRITERS

Below is a list of the scriptwriters of the Carry On films

1. Talbot Rothwell   20 films

   (Cabby, Jack, Spying*, Cleo, Cowboy, Screaming, Don't Lose Your Head, Follow That Camel, Doctor, Up the Khyber, Camping, Again Doctor, Up the Jungle, Loving, Henry, At Your Convenience, Matron, Abroad, Girls, Dick)

2. Norman Hudis   6 films

   (Sergeant, Nurse, Teacher, Constable, Regardless, Cruising)

3. Dave Freeman   2 films

   (Behind, Columbus)

4. Sid Colin   1 film
   (Spying*)
   David Pursael   1 film
   (England+)
   Jack Seddon   1 film
   (England+)
   Tony Church   1 film
   (That's Carry On)
   Lance Peters   1 film
   (Emmannuelle)

   key: *+ = co-written

Script Ratios
Number of Carry On films the two main scriptwriters wrote

1.	Talbot Rothwell	
	20 films in 12 years	60.0
2.	Norman Hudis	
	6 films in 5 years	83.3

Original scriptwriter Norman Hudis.
He wrote the first six films from 1958 to 1962.

66

THE CARRY ON TEAM BIRTHDAYS

Below is a compiled list of the birthdays of the main Carry On
team members and places of births. Now you know!

Patsy Rowlands	19th January 1934	London
Peter Butterworth	4th February 1919	Bramhall
Hattie Jacques	7th February 1924	Sandgate
Peter Rogers (producer)	20th February 1914	Rochester
Kenneth Williams	22nd February 1926	London
Bernard Bresslaw	25th February 1934	East London
Jack Douglas	26th April 1927	Newcastle
Terry Scott	4th May 1927	Watford
Sid James	8th May 1913	Johannesburg
Joan Sims	9th May 1930	Laindon
Kenneth Connor	6th June 1916	London
Norman Hudis (scriptwriter)	27th July 1922	London
Barbara Windsor	6th August 1937	Shoreditch
Jim Dale	15th August 1935	Rothwell
Alan Hume (cameraman)	16th October 1924	Putney
Talbot Rothwell (scriptwriter)	12th November 1916	Bromley
Charles Hawtrey	30th November 1934	Hounslow
Gerald Thomas (director)	10th December 1920	Hull

CARRY ON MEMORY ...

"My biggest memory is of *Carry On Camping* when I was so cold that
they had to spray the ground with green paint to look like grass and fix
leaves to the trees. Also this was the film Barbara Windsor and I
became good friends, which led to me doing *Wild Wild Women* for BBC
TV and ultimately to me getting *On The Buses* - we have remained
good friends ever since."
- *Anna Karen*

CARRY ON MEMORY ...

"Appearing in a Carry On film was like working for a family.
Peter Rogers and Gerald Thomas had assembled a group of highly
talented comedy performers, who starred regularly in these films. They
all knew one another, understood each other's timing, and a great
camaraderie existed between them. They worked at speed to get
everything filmed on time and within very strict budget limits.
A newcomer took a little time to adjust, but it was an enjoyable
experience being in one of these films."
- Nicholas Parsons

CARRY ON MEMORY ...

"The person I remember best from the Carry Ons is Bernard Bresslaw
who made his name mostly playing dim characters. He was far
removed from that in real life. He thought nothing of finishing *The
Times* crossword - the big one - in less than an hour. A delightful fellow
with a great sense of humour. His early death robbed the theatre of a
considerable actor who in later life would have had a splendid career in
the classics. He could have played practically any Shakespearean
clown. I would love to have seen his Leah."
- Harry Towb

CARRY ON MEMORY ...

"The day the England football squad came to visit the set of *Carry On
Columbus* and none of the actors broke the ice by talking to them.
I swept over in full 'Joyce Grenfell' mode (I was still playing her at
night in Re-Joyce) - "Helloooo! How lovely to meet you. May I introduce
..." etc., causing great hilarity to the rest of the much younger cast -
who then went on to become considerably more
friendly with some of the squad, than I'd anticipated."
- Maureen Lipman

CARRY ON MEMORY ...

"Working on *Carry On Nurse* was an absolute joy, very harmonious, a merry happy band of actors. The next, *Carry On Teacher,* was more problematic, not only because the work ludicrously rushed - but all the male leads were comedians or comics, and they were unable to communicate at all except by getting one up on each other by successive joke telling - maddening. Joan Sims once threatened to throw her lunch plate across the studio restaurant if another joke was told. No one took any notice - except me. The great skill of the production team of the Carry On films was that they were amazingly clever at casting. They chose people of personality who were very quick workers and fine comedians in their own right."
- Rosalind Knight

CARRY ON MEMORY ...

"*Carry On Columbus* was my one and only Carry On film. It wound up being my shortest performance ever in anything, but at least I was part of a British institution."
- Linda Baron

CARRY ON MEMORY ...

"I was only in *Carry On Henry*, my main memories are of the waiting times between filming the scenes at Pinewood Studios, when I was often regaled with ultra-enthusiastic eulogies on his beliefs about everything, from Kenneth Williams on one side of me, while Terry Scott told me jokes in between reading the *Daily Mirror*, seated on the other side of me! The contrasting approaches in their work and in life gave me great amusement. I'd worked with Sid James previously in his television series and felt a great affection for him. All the cast were friendly and I enjoyed being in the film."
- Marjie Lawrence

CARRY ON STARS' & CO-STARS' BIRTH & DEATH YEARS

Name	Born	Died	Age
Mario Fabrizi (1)	1925	1963	38
Freddie Mills (2)	1922	1965	43
Jerry Desmonde (1)	1908	1967	58
Howerd Crawford (1)	1914	1969	55
E V H Emmett (N)	1902	1971	69
Cecil Parker (1)	1897	1971	74
Kynaston Reeves (1)	1893	1971	78
Denis Shaw (1)	1921	1971	50
Esma Cannon (4)	1896	1972	76
Cyril Raymond (1)	1897	1973	76
Tony Sagar (6)	1920	1973	53
George Woodbridge (1)	1907	1973	66
Cyril Chamberlain (7)	1909	1974	65
Judith Furse (3)	1912	1974	62
William Hartnell (1)	1908	1975	63
Richard Wattis (1)	1912	1975	62
Martin Boddey (2)	1908	1976	68
Sid James (20)	1913	1976	62
William Mervyn (3)	1912	1976	64
Ted Ray (1)	1906	1977	71
Bruce Montgomery (M)	1921	1978	57
Susan Shaw (1)	1929	1978	49
Peter Butterworth (16)	1919	1979	59
Julian Orchard (4)	1930	1979	49
Sidney Tafler (1)	1916	1979	63
Eric Pohlman (2)	1903	1979	76
Imogen Hassall (1)	1942	1980	38
Renee Houston (3)	1902	1980	78
Hattie Jacques (14)	1924	1980	56
Ambrosine Philpotts (3)	1912	1980	68

Eric Rogers (M)	1913	1981	67
Talbot Rothwell (SW)	1916	1981	64
John Catrell (1)	1907	1981	73
Harry H Corbett (1)	1925	1982	57
Lucy Griffiths (6)	1919	1982	63
Norman Chappell (2)	1929	1983	54
Frances De Wolff (1)	1913	1984	71
Arnold Ridley (1)	1895	1984	89
Frank Forsyth (7)	1905	1984	79
Derek Francis (5)	1923	1984	61
Wilfred Brambell (1)	1912	1985	73
Gordon Rollings (1)	1927	1985	58
Phil Silvers (1)	1912	1985	72
Dandy Nicholls (1)	1907	1986	79
Irene Handl (2)	1901	1987	85
Harry Locke (3)	1915	1987	72
Sidney Bromley (1)	1919	1987	68
Charles Hawtrey (23)	1914	1988	73
Kenneth Williams (26)	1926	1988	62
Amelia Bayntun (5)	1919	1988	69
Robert Dorning (1)	1913	1989	76
Alan Gifford (1)	1905	1989	84
Eric Barker (4)	1912	1990	78
Jill Ireland (1)	1936	1990	54
Carol White (1)	1943	1991	48
Donald Houston (1)	1923	1991	67
Wilfred Hyde-White (1)	1903	1991	87
Percy Herbert (2)	1920	1992	72
Frankie Howerd (2)	1917	1992	75
Cardew Robinson (1)	1917	1992	74
Bob Todd (1)	1921	1992	71
Brian Oulton (4)	1908	1992	84
Bernard Bresslaw (14)	1934	1993	59
Patrick Cargill (2)	1918	1993 1996	74
Kenneth Connor (17)	1916	1993	77
Victor Maddern (5)	1928	1993	65

Gerald Thomas (D)	1920	1993	72
Roy Castle (1)	1932	1994	62
Fred Griffiths (3)	1912	1994	82
Llewellyn Rees (1)	1900	1994	94
Terry Scott (7)	1927	1994	67
Noel Dyson (2)	1916	1995	79
Dany Robin (1)	1927	1995	68
Harold Berens (1)	1903	1995	92
Peter Grant (1)	1935	1995	60
Jon Pertwee (4)	1919	1996	76
Beryl Reid (1)	1920	1996	76
Patrick Cargill (2)	1918	1996	78
Alfred Roome (E)	1907	1997	90
Michael Ward (5)	1909	1997	88
Michael Balfour (1)	1917	1997	80
Don Henderson (1)	1931	1997	66
Patricia Hayes (1)	1909	1998	88
Joan Hickson (5)	1906	1998	92
Davy Kaye (2)	1928	1998	70
James Villiers (1)	1933	1998	65
Betty Marsden (2)	1919	1998	78
Michael Nightingale (13)	1922	1998	75
Norman Rossington (3)	1928	1999	70
Bill Owen (4)	1914	1999	85
Deryck Guyler (1)	1914	1999	85
Peter Jones (2)	1920	2000	79
Brian Rowlinson (3)	1932	2000	68
Norman Mitchell (5)	1919	2001	82
Jimmy Logan (2)	1928	2001	73
Joan Sims (24)	1930	2001	71
Stanley Unwin (1)	1911	2002	90
Pat Coombs (2)	1927	2002	75
Claire Davenport (1)	1933	2002	68
Gerald Campion (1)	1921	2002	81
David Lodge (5)	1921	2003	82
Bob Monkhouse (1)	1928	2003	75

Philip Stone (1)	1924	2003	79
Larry Taylor (3)	1918	2003	84
Ed Devereaux (5)	1925	2003	78
Hilda Fenemore (2)	1919	2004	84
Michael Mellinger (1)	1930	2004	74
Molly Weir (1)	1910	2004	94
Patsy Rowlands (9)	1934	2005	71
Dave Freeman (SW)	1923	2005	82
Henry McGee (1)	1928	2006	77
Alec Bregonzi (1)	1930	2006	76
Patrick Allen (N)	1927	2006	79
Anton Rodgers (2)	1933	2007	74
Barrie Gosney (1)	1926	2008	82
Brian Wilde (1)	1922	2008	86
Jill Adams (1)	1930	2008	78
Jack Douglas (8)	1927	2008	81
Dilys Laye (4)	1935	2009	74
Wendy Richard (2)	1943	2009	65
Peter Rogers (P)	1914	2009	95
Terence Alexander(1)	1923	2009	86
Harry Towb (1)	1926	2009	83
Patrick Durkin (5)	1935	2009	74

Key = (D) Director   (P) Producer   (SW) Scriptwriter   (M) Music   (C) Cameraman   (E) Editor   (PH) Photography   (N) Narrator and all others are actors & actresses with the number of films they appeared in.

CARRY ON MEMORY ...

"*Camping* as everybody knows was made in November - in a field - at Pinewood. Wearing very little, Joan Sims and I were freezing and constantly damp. However it is one of my happiest memories working with Joan, Sid and Bernie - we laughed a lot and played a lot of poker in between showers! There was also of course the constant spraying of the leaves 'green' and the midges rose at 5pm to bite us on the legs - but we loved it!"
- Dilys Laye

CARRY ON MEMORY ...

"In *Carry On Loving* full-size real cream cakes were thrown smack into my face. After each take my blouse had to be washed then dried with a hairdryer, my make-up reapplied, and the gunge combed out of my rather expensive hairpiece ready for the next cake to be thrown by Gerald Thomas. My skin was tingling by the end of the day and I haven't been able to look a cream cake in the face since."
- Valerie Shute

CARRY ON MEMORY ...

"My memory of working on the Carry On films - one only - *Carry On England* was one of disappointment. I was disappointed that I had not appeared in them earlier! There was a great atmosphere on the set - both with the crew and artistes. It wasn't like work. It was fun. Fun, fun - all the way. To top it all, I was working with my very own Sergeant Major - Windsor Davis."
- Melvyn Hayes

CARRY ON MEMORY ...

"I have only appeared in one Carry On, *Carry On Cruising,* in which I played the ship's drunk. It was a pleasure to work with Esma Cannon, Liz Fraser and Dilys Laye."
- Ronnie Stevens

CARRY ON MEMORY ...

"*Carry On England* was one of my first jobs as a new actress. I remember clearly how helpful Kenneth Connor was to me. He gave his valuable professional time to help me learn how to be funny on camera. I was lucky enough to work with him again, when he joined the cast of *Hi De Hi*. I think he was generous with his talent and cared about people and teamwork."
- Linda Regan

CHAPTER 3
TELEVISION

ON THE BOX

The Carry On television programme series started production in 1969 and went on to run for twenty years, peaking in 1975 with 65% of the twenty programmes being televised in this year. All twenty programmes were produced between October and February. Although a spin-off from the now famous Carry On films, they never quite reached the pinnacle of success that the films reached, but still were written, produced and directed in the humorous Carry On fashion, and done extremely well.

The television productions used eleven of the main Carry On team, Kenneth Connor making eighteen appearances out of the twenty productions, a staggering 90%. The other Kenneth (Williams) never appeared in a single television programme. The only other regular team member not to appear was Jim Dale. Jack Douglas appeared in thirteen programmes in a row without missing one, some 76.5% of all seventeen he made. As in both the films and stage shows, Sid James again topped the billing orders.

A new scriptwriter, Dave Freeman, wrote almost half of the Carry On series for television and then went on to write two Carry On films, *Behind* (1975) and *Columbus* (1992).

"Get Away!"

Number one of the Carry Ons and rightly so. Peter Rogers (producer), taken 15th December 2002

CARRY ON TELEVISION
PROGRAMMES BROADCASTED

Title	Month	Year	Length	Stars	Colour/B&W
Christmas	Dec	1969	50 mins	8	Colour
Again Christmas	Dec	1970	50 mins	8	B&W
Christmas	Dec	1972	50 mins	11	Colour
What a Carry On!	Oct	1973	50 mins	6	Colour
Christmas	Dec	1973	50 mins	9	Colour
The Prisoner of Spenda	Jan	1975	21 mins	10	Colour
The Baron Outlook	Jan	1975	24 mins	12	Colour
The Sobbing Cavalier	Jan	1975	23 mins	8	Colour
Orgy and Bess	Jan	1975	23 mins	10	Colour
One in the Eye for Harold	Feb	1975	24 mins	14	Colour
The Nine Old Cobblers	Feb	1975	24 mins	9	Colour
The Case of the Screaming Winkles	Nov	1975	24 mins	11	Colour
The Case of the Coughing Parrot	Nov	1975	24 mins	10	Colour
Under the Round Table	Oct	1975	25 mins	14	Colour
Short Knights, Long Daze	Nov	1975	24 mins	11	Colour
And in My Lady's Chamber	Nov	1975	25 mins	10	Colour
Who Needs Kitchener?	Nov	1975	25 mins	10	Colour
Lamp Posts of the Empire	Dec	1975	24 mins	11	Colour
Christmas Classics	Dec	1983	24 mins	25	Colour
Norbert Smith – A Life	Nov	1989	52 mins	14	Colour

TELEVISION PROGRAMMES MADE

Years	Number	%		Months	Number	%
1975	13	65%		November	6	30%
1973	2	10%		December	6	30%
1969	1	5%		January	4	20%
1970	1	5%		February	2	10%
1972	1	5%		October	2	10%
1983	1	5%				
1989	1	5%				

Averages

Stars 221 = 11 in each programme

Running time total 636 minutes = average of 31.8 minutes per show

95% filmed in colour, 5% filmed in B&W

CARRY ON MEMORY ...

"During *Carry On Sergeant* I was booked for *Carry On Nurse*. Peter Rogers wanted me to play a crossed-eyed person. After two weeks he said I was to be crossed in one eye. I practised for weeks and finally managed to cross just one eye. On the day we started filming *Nurse* he said 'Forget it Ed, we want you to play a man who is impotent'! Peter's little joke!"

- Ed Devereaux

CARRY ON MEMORY ...

"I appeared in two Carry On films, *Again Doctor* and *Up the Jungle*. I was only a small cog in a much bigger wheel, however the cast of the two films I worked on were lovely people who showed much kindness to a novice, especially Sid James."

- Heather Emmanuel

CARRY ON TELEVISION APPEARANCES

Listed below is a league of the top twelve television appearances by the stars

		Number	Percentage
1.	Kenneth Connor	18	90%
2.	Jack Douglas	17	85%
3.	Barbara Windsor	15	75%
4.	Peter Butterworth	14	70%
	Joan Sims		
5.	Bernard Bresslaw	9	45%
	Sid James		
6.	Brian Osborne	8	40%
7.	Norman Chappell	7	35%
	David Lodge		
8.	John Carlin	6	30%
9.	Sherrie Hewson	5	25%
10.	Billy Cornelius	4	20%
	Hattie Jacques		
11.	Carol Hawkins	3	15%
	Charles Hawtrey		
	Vivienne Johnson		
	Diane Langton		
	Victor Maddern		
	Terry Scott		
12.	Brian Capron	2	10%
	Julian Holloway		
	Linda Hooks		
	Frankie Howerd		
	Oscar James		
	Valerie Leon		
	Desmond McNamara		
	Michael Nightingale		
	Andrew Ray		
	Patsy Rowlands		
	Ronnie Brody		

Also other stars like Johnny Briggs, Harry Enfield, Laraine Humphreys, Marianne Stone and Melvyn Hayes made appearances in Carry On TV and who also had an association with the films.

SUSTAINED APPEARANCES IN CARRY ON TELEVISION

These are the top six sustained appearances in the Carry On television series by the stars without missing a programme. (Compiled from 1969 to 1989)

1. Jack Douglas   13   65%
   (from *The Sobbing Cavalier* to *Norbert Smith – A Life*)

2. Kenneth Connor   12   60%
   (from *Orgy and Bess* to *Norbert Smith – A Life*)

3. Barbara Windsor   9   45%
   (from *Christmas '69* to *Orgy and Bess*)

4. Joan Sims   8   40%
   (from *One in the Eye for Harold* to *Who Needs Kitchener?*)

5. Bernard Bresslaw   6   30%
   (from *Under the Round Table* to *Laughing Christmas Classics*)
   Peter Butterworth
   (from *Christmas '72* to *The Sobbing Cavalier*)
   Sid James
   (from *What a Carry On!* to *Orgy And Bess*)

6. John Carlin   4   20%
   (from *Orgy and Bess* to *The Case of the Screaming Winkles*)
   Norman Chappell
   (from *The Case of the Screaming Winkles* to *Short Knight, Long Daze*)
   David Lodge
   (from *One in the Eye for Harold* to *The Case of the Coughing Parrot*)
   Brian Osborne
   (from *The Baron Outlook* to *One in the Eye for Harold*)

CARRY ON TELEVISION
LEAGUE OF BILLING ORDERS*

1.	Sid James	1.0		7.	Jack Douglas	3.6
2.	Terry Scott	2.0		8.	Peter Butterworth	4.5
3.	Hattie Jacques	2.3		9.	Bernard Bresslaw	5.0
4.	Kenneth Connor	2.6		10.	Patsy Rowlands	7.0
5.	Barbara Windsor	2.9		11.	Frankie Howerd	8.0
6.	Charles Hawtrey	3.0				
	Joan Sims	3.0				

* Does not include *Carry On Christmas* classics as appeared in alphabetical order in the billing.

CARRY ON MEMORY ...

"I only have happy memories of the Carry On films. The main team all seemed very comfortable together and were very friendly to us. I remember putting my foot down about wearing a see-through costume on *Carry On Dick* and four of us 'won the day'!"
- *Laraine Humphreys*

CARRY ON MEMORY ...

"I do remember how nervous I was on my first day on a Carry On set, until the lovely Kenneth Williams, understanding how I was feeling, screamed from one end of the hospital ward, 'Oh yes, you don't want to know me now, do you?' and greeted me like an old friend (which I wasn't). It broke the ice and I loved him for it."
- *Marianne Stone*

CARRY ON TELEVISION
BILLING ORDERS*

Sid James	1,1,1,1,1,1,1,1	8
Terry Scott	2,2	4
Charles Hawtrey	3,3	6
Hattie Jacques	4,1,2	7
Barbara Windsor	5,5,3,2,3,2,3,3,4,3,2,2,1,3	41
Bernard Bresslaw	6,6,5,4,4,6,5,4	40
Peter Butterworth	7,5,4,5,3,4,5,4,6,3,3,5,5	59
Frankie Howerd	8	8
Kenneth Connor	4,4,3,4,5,3,2,2,2,2,1,1,1,1	35
Joan Sims	2,2,4,2,4,3,4,3,3,2,2,4,4	39
Jack Douglas	7,6,7,6,2,5,1,1,1,1,5,5,3,3,3,2	58
Patsy Rowlands	7	7

* Does not include *Carry On Christmas* classics as appeared in alphabetical order in the billing.

CARRY ON MEMORY ...
"It was a great privilege to be included in the Carry On legend, through the television series. It was a fun job with fun people and as a young actress it was exciting to be part of the very famous rogues gallery of British comedy. We covered various spoofs from *Upstairs Downstairs* to *The Case of the Coughing Parrot*! Loosely based on Sherlock Holmes, if my memory serves me correctly, with lots of dry ice mystery!"
- *Vivienne Johnson*

CARRY ON MEMORY ...
"It was such a long time ago - but I remember the fun we had working on *Carry On Cabby*. The whole team were all so kind to me, especially Sid James."
- *Milo O'Shea*

CARRY ON TELEVISION WRITERS

The league of television scriptwriters

	Name	Number Written	Percentage
1.	Dave Freeman	9	45%
	(Again Christmas+, Christmas*, Prisoner Of Spenda, Baron Outlook, Sobbing Cavalier, Nine Old Cobblers, Case of the Screaming Winkles, Case of the Coughing Parrot, Christmas Classics#)		
2.	Lew Scharz	6	30%
	(One in the Eye for Harold, Under the Round Table, Short Knight, Long Daze, And in My Lady's Chamber, Who Needs Kitchener?, Lamp Posts of the Empire)		
3.	Talbot Rothwell	4	20%
	(Christmas 1969, Christmas 1972, Christmas 1973, Christmas Classics#)		
4.	Sid Colin	1	5%
	(Again Christmas+)		
	Barry Cryer	1	5%
	(Orgy and Bess>)		
	Dick Vosburgh	1	5%
	(Orgy and Bess>)		
	Harry Enfield	1	5%
	(Norbert Smith – A Life<)		
	Geoff Perkins	1	5%
	(Norbert Smith – A Life<)		

key: + * # > < = co-written

CARRY ON MEMORY ...

"When I was offered *Carry On Columbus* I agreed instantly. I was not going to turn down the chance to be part of an institution like the Carry Ons. It was great to meet up again with cameraman Alan Hume, with whom I had worked on several projects previously. I had a delightful time working with Rik Mayall and Nigel Planer. In all, a fun job, as I had expected."

- Burt Kwouk

THE PEOPLE BEHIND THE SCENES

The people who worked behind the scenes on the Carry On television programmes are listed below

Title	Number worked on	Percentage
Graphics		
George Wallder	13	65%
Animator		
Len Lewis	11	55%
Sound		
Len Penfold	7	35%
Cameras		
Mike Whitcutt	7	35%
Make-up		
Sheila Mann	7	35%
Wardrobe		
James Dark	7	35%
Executive Producer/Producer		
Gerald Thomas	16	80%
Peter Rogers	16	80%
Peter Eton	2	10%
Geoffrey Perkins	2	10%
Director		
Allan Tarrant	14	70%
Ronnie Baxter	2	10%
Ronald Fouracre	1	5%
David Clark	1	5%
Geoff Posner	1	5%
Designer		
Richard Lake	3	15%
Roger Allen	2	10%
Ray White	2	10%
Lewis Logan	2	10%
Brian Holgate	2	10%
Anthony Walker	2	10%

CHAPTER 4
STAGE

TREADING THE BOARDS

After producing twenty five successful Carry On films and four successful television programmes, the "Rogers and Thomas" partnership tried their luck at carrying on in the theatre. Immediately after finishing *Carry On Girls* on 25th May 1973, Peter Rogers assembled six of his regular team for the stage show *Carry On London*. It was initially performed at The Birmingham Hippodrome between 14th and 29th September 1973. It worked - who would have doubted it, as anything with the Carry On logo attached to it would work anywhere.

So the production moved on to The Victoria Palace, London, where it was directed by the late Bill Roberton, brother of Carry On star Jack Douglas. The show ran for almost a year and a half. Two more successful shows followed, both in the summer seasons of 1975 and 1992, in Scarborough and Blackpool respectively.

It took fifty-two production staff to produce the three Carry On hit stage shows, with also fourteen companies involved in supplying their services.

Carry On showing "Ooh matron"

CARRY ON MEMORY ...

"As a starring young actor in *Under the Round Table*, I played the role of The Black Knight. I was asked if I could ride a horse so I said, 'Yes of course'. In fact I hadn't even sat on one, but I needed the money. So, dressed in armour and carrying a jousting stick, the horse bolted off with me clinging on for dear life! I was just about to throw myself off before I came to a sticky end, when the director shouted 'Cut' and the trainer came to my rescue. I found out later that it was an ex-RACEHORSE!"
- Oscar James

CARRY ON STAGE SHOWS

The three Carry On stage shows that were performed were:

1. **Carry On London** from 4.10.73 to 31.3.75
(The Victoria Palace, London) (2 acts – duration 2 hours 30 mins)

The Sketches

Act 1	Act 2
Round about Victoria!!	Carry On London
What a Carry On!	Hello Dollies
Carry On Girls	Be Prepared
Emergency Ward 99 and a bit	Cleopatra's Palace on the Nile
Deauville 1900	Cleopatra's Boudoir
Elizabethan Madrigals	Smile
London Night Out	
Curtain time at the Royal Standard Music Hall	

2. **Carry On Laughing** with **The Slimming Factory** from 16.6.75 to
30.9.75 (Royal Opera House, Scarborough) (2 acts – duration 2 hours
35 mins) A Play based on the residents of the Get-U-Fit Health Farm

The Sketches

Act 1	Act 2
Scene 1 Monday Morning	Thursday Afternoon
Scene 2 Wednesday Morning	Thursday Night

3. **Wot a Carry On in Blackpool** from 22.5.92 to 25.10.92
(The North Pier, Blackpool) (2 acts – duration 2 hours 30 mins)

The Sketches

Act 1	Act 2
Arrival	It's Show Time
Rehearsals	London Medley
Out of Town just go to the Movies	Wot a Carry On

87

CARRY ON STAGE APPEARANCES

The team league of stage appearances

1.   Barbara Windsor   2   66.7%
     (London, Wot a Carry On in Blackpool)
     Kenneth Connor   2   66.7%
     (London, Carry On Laughing with The Slimming Factory)
     Peter Butterworth   2   66.7%
     (London, Carry On Laughing with The Slimming Factory)
     Bernard Bresslaw   2   66.7%
     (London, Wot a Carry On In Blackpool)
     Jack Douglas   2   66.7%
     (London, Carry On Laughing with The Slimming Factory)

2.   Sid James   1   33.3%
     (London)
     Liz Fraser   1   33.3%
     (Carry On Laughing with The Slimming Factory)
     Linda Hooks   1   33.3%
     (Carry On Laughing with The Slimming Factory)
     Anne Aston   1   33.3%
     (Carry On Laughing with The Slimming Factory)

CARRY ON STAGE BILLING ORDERS

Sid James	1	1
Barbara Windsor	2,2	4
Kenneth Connor	3,2	5
Peter Butterworth	4,3	7
Bernard Bresslaw	5,1	6
Jack Douglas	6,1	7
Liz Fraser	4	4

CARRY ON STAGE
LEAGUE OF BILLING ORDERS

As in both the films and television billings Sid James again comes out on top in the stage billings. He was with no doubt the anchorman in the entire Carry On series. While appearing in *Carry On London* at the Victoria Palace, Sid and fellow team members Barbara Windsor, Kenneth Connor, Bernard Bresslaw, Peter Butterworth and Jack Douglas were also making *Carry On Dick* in March and April of 1974 - what dedication to the Carry Ons!

1.	Sid James	1.0
2.	Barbara Windsor	2.0
3.	Kenneth Connor	2.5
4.	Bernard Bresslaw	3.0
5.	Peter Butterworth	3.5
	Jack Douglas	3.5
6.	Liz Fraser	4.0

Jack Douglas

JACK DOUGLAS
Jack entered the team very late, in fact in 1971, with a small role in *Matron* and stayed until *Columbus*. He was instantly accepted by all fellow members, and went on to star in a number of Carry On television specials and two Carry On stage shows. Jack is one of only a few to star in both film, television and stage versions of the Carry Ons.

CARRY ON MEMORY ...
"I only did one Carry On film - *Carry On Regardless* and I worked on it for four days, so I'm afraid I have no cheerful reflections, although everyone was very nice and poor old Freddie Mills was charming."
- Terence Alexander

CARRY ON STAGE WRITERS

	Name	Number written	Percentage
1.	Sam Cree	1	100%
	(Carry On Laughing with The Slimming Factory)		
2.	Barry Cryer	1*	50%
	(Wot a Carry On in Blackpool)		
	Dick Vosburgh	1*	50%
	(Wot a Carry On in Blackpool)		
3.	Talbot Rothwell	1#	33.3%
	(London)		
	Dave Freeman	1#	33.3%
	(London)		
	Eric Merriman	1#	33.3%
	(London)		

key: #* = co-written

Only two Carry On scriptwriters were involved in both film, television and stage productions. They were Talbot Rothwell and Dave Freeman who between them had written thirty-seven out of fifty-four productions, amounting to 68.5% of all Carry Ons. With original film scriptwriter Norman Hudis, the figure rises to an astonishing 79.6% – well that's a hell of a lot of writing!

CARRY ON MEMORY ...
"One day after lunch on the set of Carry On Nurse Charles Hawtrey (who enjoyed a drink or two) tripped over an electric cable and fell on top of Peter Rogers, the producer. Rogers glared up at him from the floor and said, 'Pissed'. Hawtrey smiled benignly from his position astride the producer and replied, 'So am I!"
- Patrick Durkin

STAGE SHOWS
THE PEOPLE BEHIND THE SCENES

Job description	Number worked on	Percentage
Director		
Bill Roberton	2	66.7%
Tudor Davies	1	33.3%
Stage Director/Manager		
Alan West	1	33.3%
Tommy Layton	1	33.3%
Sharon Curtis	1	33.3%
Manager		
Alan West	1	33.3%
John Palmer	1	33.3%
Peter Waters	1	33.3%
Designer		
Tod Kingman	1	33.3%
Saxon Lucas	1	33.3%
Gareth Bowen	1	33.3%
Wardrobe		
Eve Barnes	1	33.3%
Judi Kingman	1	33.3%
Heidi Wynter	1	33.3%
Choreography		
Tommy Shaw	1	50.0%
Paul Robinson	1	50.0%

CARRY ON MEMORY ...

"It was so long ago, I can only recall the main events that happened. It was my second television job since leaving RADA in 1968. I was at the Birmingham Rep; the 'old rep' as it is now called. At that time the Artistic Director was Peter Dews, a wonderful director and a great teacher of young actors. For this particular episode I was to play and sing the links between the various scenes, a sort of wandering minstrel. When the day arrived for filming my 'wandering', it was pouring with rain! So I did most of the scenes leaning nonchalantly in covered doorways or under thick trees. I met Bernard Bresslaw, who I think was directing, and he was very kind and generous to this young actor. On reflection I am glad that I was young when I did it. The thought now of composing and playing the guitar - I had only just begun to learn this instrument - would be pretty daunting. There was such a good atmosphere on the location that one could hardly fail. Wonderful times. I loved the Carry On television and film series. Uncompromisingly English."

- Desmond McNamara

The ballroom which adjoins the theatre - Pinewood Studios.
Final scene used in Carry On Loving (1970) and the Carry On Conventions

CHAPTER 5
OVERALL

WHAT? ALL THAT!

Undoubtedly the most famous name to us, the general public, was the lovable Sid James – also known as the anchorman within the Carry On team. He holds the record for top billing in the Carry On films, and television and stage productions.

"Cor blimey!"

In 1971 a new member joined the Carry On team by the name of Jack Douglas. He was instantly accepted by all former members. Jack ranks at number five in the overall list of appearances, with an astonishing twenty-eight to his credit, quite a feat for someone joining the team fourteen years into the series.

"Wuhey Give Over!"

Kenneth Williams holds the record with twenty-six appearances out of thirty-one films. The top female performer in the films was Joan Sims with twenty-four to her credit. She also holds the record for sustained appearances with twenty-one films on the trot. Charles Hawtrey made the most number of films in the least number of years, twenty-three films in fifteen years.

Kenneth Connor tops the television appearances with eighteen, a staggering 90% of programmes produced.

"Ooh Matron!"

Outside of the mansion house in Pinewood Studios, scene used in Carry On Again Doctor (1969)

CARRY ONS MADE

The total of all the Carry Ons ever made

Films	31	57.4%
Television shows	20	37.0%
Stage shows	3	5.6%
Total	54	100.0%

CARRY ON MEMORY ...

"What memories do I have of the films which changed my life? Plenty. To isolate just one: going along the London street which housed the Carlton Cinema and seeing people queueing for *Carry On Nurse*. Limited to a few lines here, I now craftily refer you, for fuller reminiscence, to my book *No Laughing Matter*, from the same Carry On-friendly publisher, Apex!"
- *Norman Hudis*

THE BIG THREE

Overall scriptwriters

		Film/TV & Stage	Average
1.	Talbot Rothwell	20,4,1	8.3
2.	Dave Freeman	2,9,1	4.0
3.	Norman Hudis	6,0,0	2.0

OVERALL CARRY ON APPEARANCES FOR FILMS, TV AND STAGE

1.	Joan Sims	38	70.4%
2.	Kenneth Connor	37	68.5%
3.	Peter Butterworth	32	59.3%
4.	Sid James	29	53.7%
5.	Jack Douglas	28	51.9%
6.	Kenneth Williams	27	50.0%
	Barbara Windsor		
7.	Charles Hawtrey	26	48.1%
8.	Bernard Bresslaw	25	46.3%
9.	Hattie Jacques	18	33.3%
10.	Michael Nightingale	12	22.2%
11.	Jim Dale	11	20.4%
	Patsy Rowlands		
12.	Julian Holloway	10	18.5%
	Terry Scott		
	Peter Gilmore		
13.	Marianne Stone	9	16.6%
14.	Valerie Leon	8	14.8%

In the Carry On films Charles Hawtrey ranks third – if it wasn't for arguments over his billing order with producer Peter Rogers he would have been top of the league, as other stars such as Kenneth Williams and Joan Sims were contracted to other work, which left them out of various Carry On films. Why argue over the billing orders when you could have topped the Carry On star league? A lot of people would have given their right arm to head such a list of celebrities in the best comedy film series in the world, but instead the honour went to Kenneth Williams.

OVERALL BILLING RUNNING ORDERS

Listed below are the overall billing running orders for the
Carry On films, television and stage productions

		Film/TV & Stage	*Average*
1.	Sid James	1,1,1	1.0
2.	Kenneth Williams	2,0,0	2.0
3.	Kenneth Connor	4,4,3	3.6
4.	Jim Dale	4,0,0	4.0
5.	Barbara Windsor	6,5,2	4.3
6.	Charles Hawtrey	3,6,0	4.5
7.	Hattie Jacques	7,3,0	5.0
8.	Joan Sims Terry Scott	5,6,0 9,2,0	5.5 5.5
9.	Bernard Bresslaw	7,9,4	6.6
10.	Peter Butterworth	8,8,5	7.0
11.	Jack Douglas	10,7,5	7.3
12.	Patsy Rowlands	11,10,0	10.5

CARRY ON FILMS RELEASED BY:

1.   Rank Organisation   17   54.8%
      (from *Don't Lose Your Head* to *That's Carry On*, films 13 to 29)

2.   Anglo Amalgamated   12   38.7%
      (from *Sergeant* to *Screaming*, films 1 to 12)

3.   Hemdale   1   3.2%
      (*Emmannuelle*, film 30)
      Island World   1   3.2%
      (*Columbus*, film 31)

CARRY ON TV PROGRAMMES PRODUCTION BY:

1.   ATV Network   14   70%
      (*Wot a Carry On*, programme 4, from *The Prisoner of Spenda* to
      Lamp-Posts of the Empire, programmes 6 to 18)

2.   Thames   5   25%
      (from *Christmas 1969* to *Christmas 1972*, programmes 1 to 3
      Christmas 1973, programme 5 and *Christmas Classics*, programme 19)

3.   Channel 4   1   5%
      (*Norbert Smith – A Life*, programme 20)

CARRY ON STAGE SHOWS PRESENTED BY:

1.   Louis Benjamin   1   33.3%
      (*The Peter Rogers Production*)
      (*Carry On London*)
      Don Robinson   1   33.3%
      (in association with Peter Rogers and Gerald Thomas)
      (*Carry On Laughing with The Slimming Factory*)
      Mike Hughes   1   33.3%
      (Liver Productions Ltd)
      (*Wot a Carry On in Blackpool*)

CHAPTER 6
THE PRODUCTION (FILMS)

A PEEP BEHIND THE SCENES

While you sit watching the hilarious Carry On films, has it ever crossed your mind what went into producing one of the films? In this chapter of the book we look at some interesting statistics and technical data from the films, which enable you the fan to get an insight into those elusive production notes, which have been held at the British Film Institute, London, since 1992. After the completion of the final film in the series, *Carry On Columbus*, Gerald Thomas (director) sent all of the production notes from all thirty films from Pinewood Studios to the Institute where they are stored for future authors to use as a research source information to put into new Carry On books like this.

The boxes contain interesting correspondence from the stars and also contracts from Adder Productions, who dealt with the financial agreements. For every box of production papers there is also a box of original scripts to the films. What follows makes very interesting reading for the fan.

"I Only Arsked!"

*Sir Donald Sinden CBE unveiling a plaque to celebrate Peter Rogers' 50 years
in the film business at Pinewood Studios, on the 29th April 2001*

FILMING THE CARRY ONS

The shooting schedule on the Carry Ons was always the same, six five-day weeks, eight and a half hours per day, never any overtime.

The camera equipment was basic: one 35mm NC Mitchell camera with six lenses, ranging from 18mm to 75mm, plus zoom lens 20mm to 200mm, together with the usual tripods and heads for panning and tilting the camera, also what is called a 'dolly' – for tracking the camera around as and when required. A small hand-held camera would also be used for picking up odd close-ups and action shots. The usual shooting procedure was as follows:

Gerald Thomas would walk the scene through with the actors on set, so that the camera and sound crew could mark the floor for the actors' positions, and also the relevant camera positions. When this was done Gerald would usually sit with the actors and rehearse the dialogue.

Whilst this was happening, the camera and lighting crew would get the shot set-up and lit. We would average around twenty set-ups per day, very seldom doing more than two to three takes. Sometimes we would need to shoot more takes, almost always due to the actors creating convulsive laughter both in front of and behind the camera. It was always great fun working on a Carry On movie and it was a real pleasure to be at work.

The films were always tightly scheduled, efficiently prepared and well organised by their producer Peter Rogers.

Gerald was an expert editor and knew exactly what he wanted to shoot in the way of long shots, medium shots and close-ups, always giving himself plenty of options for finally editing each scene. His great competence as a director was responsible for there being a happy atmosphere on the shooting set. I have nothing but happy memories of the time I spent while shooting sixteen Carry On films.

Alan Hume
Cameraman & Director of Photography

PINEWOOD STUDIOS
THE STAGES USED IN THE PRODUCTION
OF THE CARRY ON FILMS

Eight different stages were used in the production of the thirty Carry On films. While researching some notes I came across a list of these and their sizes to give the fan an idea of the space required when making a set for a scene in the films.

Large stages

A	165 feet x 110 feet	18,150 square feet
D	165 feet x 110 feet	18,150 square feet
E	165 feet x 110 feet	18,150 square feet

Medium stages

B	110 feet x 82 feet	9,020 square feet
C	110 feet x 82 feet	9,020 square feet

Small stages

F	54 feet x 50 feet	2,700 square feet
G	57 feet x 80 feet	4,560 square feet
H	57 feet x 57 feet	3,249 square feet

Inside of Sound Stage D, one of the largest stages used in the making of the Carry On films

The Orchard at Pinewood Studios, scene used in Carry On Camping (1968), Carry On Behind (1975) and Carry On England (1976)

The parade ground, Queens Barracks, Stoughton, Guildford – location used in Carry On Sergeant (1958)

Sound Stage H at Pinewood Studios, one of the small stages used in the making of the Carry On films. This stage is the oldest in use at Pinewood and is soon to be replaced

Slough Town Hall – location used as the Council Hall in Carry On Girls (1973)

Drayton Secondary School, Ealing – location used in Carry On Teacher (1959)

CARRY ON SERGEANT - 1958

The first film of the series, featuring William Hartnell, who later went on to *Doctor Who* fame in the 1960s. Set in the army barracks of Heathercrest Service Depot, a group of recruits join up to serve their country in National Service to create a champion platoon, - very able! Besides Hartnell, this was also Bob Monkhouse and Dora Bryan's only appearance in a Carry On film.

Data	Main Team Billings	Production Staff
Film: B&W	1. Kenneth Connor	Male: 16
Format: Feature Film	2. Charles Hawtrey	Female: 4
Standard Projection: 24 fps	3. Kenneth Williams	
Running Time: 1 hr 23 mins	4. Hattie Jacques	Film Started: Mar 1958
Gauge: 35mm	5. Terry Scott	Film Finished: May 1958
Aspect Ratio: 1.75		Film Released: Aug 1958
Certificate: U		Locations Used: 3
Reels: 10		

CARRY ON NURSE - 1958

The first medical drama of the film series. Set on a ward, the story follows a selection of patients through their stay in hospital, being cared for by the delightful Shirley Eaton, in the second of her three Carry On films. This film includes the hilarious laughing gas scene when trying to operate Leslie Phillips' bunion, and also the colonel played by Wilfred Hyde-White who ends up with his temperature being taken by a daffodil in the most peculiar place. Over 2,000,000 plastic daffodils were imported from Japan to advertise this film, and it certainly did the trick, with *Nurse* being a cult film on the American campuses.

Data	Main Team Billings	Production Staff
Film: B&W	1. Kenneth Connor	Male: 17
Format: Feature Film	2. Charles Hawtrey	Female: 4
Standard Projection: 24 fps	3. Kenneth Williams	
Running Time: 1 hr 26 mins	4. Hattie Jacques	Film Started: Nov 1958
Gauge: 35mm	5. Joan Sims	Film Finished: Dec 1958
Aspect Ratio: 1.75		Film Released: Mar 1959
Certificate: U		Locations Used: 2
Reels: 10		

CARRY ON TEACHER - 1959

Ted Ray's one and only appearance in a Carry On film, as Mr Wakefield, the headmaster of Maudlin Street School. Set around a gang of children intent on giving the school a bad name, thus stopping Mr Wakefield leaving at the end of term. The gang includes a young Richard O'Sullivan who later went on to *Man About The House* and *Robin's Nest* fame in the 1970s. This film sees the Carry On team at their best in the third film of the series.

Data	Main Team Billings	Production Staff
Film: B&W	1. Kenneth Connor	Male: 13
Format: Feature Film	2. Charles Hawtrey	Female: 4
Standard Projection: 24 fps	3. Kenneth Williams	
Running Time: 1 hr 26 mins	4. Hattie Jacques	Film Started: Mar 1959
Gauge: 35mm	5. Joan Sims	Film Finished: Apr 1959
Aspect Ratio: 1.75		Film Released: Aug 1959
Certificate: U		Locations Used: 1
Reels: 10		

CARRY ON CONSTABLE - 1959

The fourth film in the series and the introduction of legend, Sid James, as Sergeant Frank Wilkins (156), in charge of the new recruits from the police training schools, which include Leslie Phillips as Constable Tom Potter (129), none hotter. One of the Hertfordshire Potters, he arrives for duty complete with tennis racquet under his arm. Filmed in Ealing, West London and, of course, Pinewood Studios, one of Norman Hudis's finest, bringing out the old cops and robbers chase scene, and ending with the recruits victorious, which kept Sergeant Wilkins his job and thus enowed his promotion.

Data	Main Team Billings	Production Staff
Film: B&W	1. Sid James	Male: 12
Format: Feature Film	2. Kenneth Connor	Female: 5
Standard Projection: 24 fps	3. Charles Hawtrey	
Running Time: 1 hr 26 mins	4. Kenneth Williams	Film Started: Nov 1959
Gauge: 35mm	5. Joan Sims	Film Finished: Dec 1959
Aspect Ratio: 1.75	6. Hattie Jacques	Film Released: Feb 1960
Certificate: U		Locations Used: 7
Reels: 10		

CARRY ON REGARDLESS - 1960

Based around the Helping Hands agency headed by Bert Handy, played by Sid James, this film sees the team up to all sorts of tasks: Kenneth Williams taking Yoki the chimpanzee for a walk and trying to hail a cab, with the cabby saying, "I'll take you, but not your mate!" This line wasn't written by Norman Hudis, but was a great piece of improvisation by the London cabby. *Regardless* was Norman's least favourite of the six films he had scripted. It was filmed in Park Street, Windsor, where the same street was used for *Loving* ten years later.

Data	Main Team Billings	Production Staff
Film: B&W	1. Sid James	Male: 13
Format: Feature Film	2. Kenneth Connor	Female: 4
Standard Projection: 24 fps	3. Charles Hawtrey	
Running Time: 1 hr 30 mins	4. Kenneth Williams	Film Started: Nov 1960
Gauge: 35mm	5. Joan Sims	Film Finished: Jan 1961
Aspect Ratio: 1.75	6. Hattie Jacques	Film Released: Mar 1961
Certificate: U		Locations Used: 4
Total Scenes: 1,153		
Reels: 10		

CARRY ON CRUISING - 1962

Cruising was the first film to be filmed in colour. New recruits joined the SS Happy Wanderer as part of Captain Wellington Crowther's well-established crew. This filmed was totally filmed on the sound stages at Pinewood Studios - the team were hoping for sunnier locations but it wasn't to be. The opening shot of the ship is filmed at Southampton docks. Lance Percival stood in for Charles Hawtrey when he became unavailable.

Data	Main Team Billings	Production Staff
Film: Colour	1. Sid James	Male: 17
Format: Feature Film	2. Kenneth Williams	Female: 5
Standard Projection: 24 fps	3. Kenneth Connor	
Running Time: 1 hr 29 mins		Film Started: Jan 1962
Gauge: 35mm		Film Finished: Feb 1962
Aspect Ratio: 1.75		Film Released: Apr 1962
Certificate: U		Locations Used: 1
Reels: 10		

CARRY ON CABBY - 1963

Cabby was the first film in the series written by Talbot (Tolly) Rothwell. It reportedly took him just two weeks to come up with the script for this masterpiece. The film also saw the first appearance of Jim Dale, who was recommended by Kenneth Williams, and introduced him into the Carry On fold. He went on to make another nine films. Cabby was filmed in and around Windsor. It remains one of the true classics of the ever-popular Carry Ons.

Data
Film: B&W
Format: Feature Film
Standard Projection: 24 fps
Running Time: 1 hr 31 mins
Gauge: 35mm
Aspect Ratio: 1.75
Certificate: U
Total Scenes Used: 262
Stills Produced: 264
Stills Published: 122
Reels: 10

Main Team Billings
1. Sid James
2. Hattie Jacques
3. Charles Hawtrey
4. Kenneth Connor
5. Jim Dale

Production Staff
Male: 18
Females: 3

Film Started: Mar 1963
Film Finished: May 1963
Film Released: June 1963
Locations Used: 6

CARRY ON JACK - 1963

This film is sheer pantomime, as Peter Rogers described it. Set on the good ship *Venus*, it follows the four crew members via Spain and back to England, recapturing their beloved *Venus* on the way. Juliet Mills made her only appearance of the series in this film. It reportedly took half a day to film the opening scene, 'Kiss Me Hardy'. Bernard Cribbins was introduced being taken into Dirty Dicks where he was told to wave a gold coin in the air to show his intentions were honourable. The Spanish coast scenes were filmed at Frensham Ponds in Surrey.

Data
Film: Colour
Format: Feature Film
Standard Projection: 24 fps
Running Time: 1 hr 31 mins
Gauge: 35mm
Aspect Ratio: 1.75
Certificate: A
Total Scenes: 976
Reels: 10

Main Team Billings
1. Kenneth Williams
2. Charles Hawtrey
3. Jim Dale

Production Staff
Male: 16
Female: 3

Film Started: Sept 1963
Film Finished: Oct 1963
Film Released: Nov 1963
Locations Used: 1

107

CARRY ON CABBY - 1963

*Listed below is a breakdown of where and how many
scenes were shot for this classic*

Date	Pinewood stage/location	Number of scenes
25.3.63	C	9
26.3.63	C	2
27.3.63	C	6
28.3.63	Lot	4
29.3.63	C	4
1.4.63	Lot	7
2.4.63	C & Lot	16
3.4.63	Location (Windsor)	13
4.4.63	Location (Windsor)	8
5.4.63	Windsor & C & Lot	3
8.4.63	Location (Windsor)	10
9.4.63	Location (Windsor)	11
10.4.63	C	6
11.4.63	C	7
16.4.63	C	4
17.4.63	A & C	4
18.4.63	Lot	3
19.4.63	Lot	8 (Night)
23.4.63	Lot & C	8
24.4.63	C	16
25.4.63	Location (Windsor)	6
26.4.63	Location (Windsor)	11
29.4.63	A	13
30.4.63	Location (Windsor)	15
1.5.63	A	7
2.5.63	Location & A	12
3.5.63	A	10
6.5.63	A	16
7.5.63	A	24
8.5.63	Lot	5

CARRY ON SPYING - 1964

This film, a spoof of the popular James Bond films was to introduce Barbara Windsor into the Carry On series, . It was the last film to be made in black and white, and the whole film was shot at Pinewood Studios in the heart of Buckinghamshire. The four bumbling agents, who included Charlie Bind agent oh, oh, oh, make their way across Europe and North Africa in pursuit of a formula, that Milchman, played by Victor Maddern, had stolen from the laboratory in the opening scene.

Data	Main Team Billings	Production Staff
Film: B&W	1. Kenneth Williams	Male: 17
Format: Feature Film	2. Barbara Windsor	Female: 4
Standard Projection: 24 fps	3. Charles Hawtrey	
Running Time: 1 hr 27 mins	4. Jim Dale	Film Started: Feb 1964
Gauge: 35mm		Film Finished: Mar 1964
Aspect Ratio: 1.75		Film Released: Jun 1964
Certificate: A		Locations Used: 1
Reels: 10		

CARRY ON CLEO - 1964

"Friends, Romans, Countrymen, I know": words uttered by Kenneth Williams as Julius Caesar throughout the film. Made just after the Burton and Taylor *Cleopatra*, Peter Rogers actually used some of the same set before it was dismantled, thus keeping down the production costs and enabling another film to be produced within budget. Amanda Barrie of Coronation Street fame starred in her second and final Carry On with Sid James in his fifth film of the series taking a bite of her asp.

Data	Main Team Billings	Production Staff
Film: Colour	1. Sid James	Male: 15
Format: Feature Film	2. Kenneth Williams	Female: 3
Standard Projection: 24 fps	3. Charles Hawtrey	
Running Time: 1 hr 32 mins	4. Kenneth Connor	Film Started: July 1964
Gauge: 35mm	5. Joan Sims	Film Finished: Aug 1964
Aspect Ratio: 1.75	6. Jim Dale	Film Released: Nov 1964
Certificate: A		Locations Used: 1
Reels: 10		

CARRY ON COWBOY - 1965

A fine performance by Angela Douglas as Annie Oakley in the first of her four Carry Ons. She grabs the attention of The Rumpo Kid, played by Sid James, who owns the boozing den Rumpo's Place. Helped by Marshal P. Knutt (Jim Dale) the sanitary engineer, Annie comes to Stodge City to avenge her father's death. Kenneth Williams, as Judge Burke, and Joan Sims as Belle, put on their American accents in the take-off of the cowboy and Indian era. In the final scenes Marshal P. Knutt uses the drains to his advantage to kill off Rumpo's gang.

Data	Main Team Billings	Production Staff
Film: Colour	1. Sid James	Male: 18
Format: Feature Film	2. Kenneth Williams	Female: 3
Standard Projection: 24 fps	3. Jim Dale	
Running Time: 1 hr 35 mins	4. Charles Hawtrey	Film Started: July 1965
Gauge: 35mm	5. Joan Sims	Film Finished: Sep 1965
Aspect Ratio: 1.75	6. Peter Butterworth	Film Released: Nov 1965
Certificate: A	7. Bernard Bresslaw	Locations Used: 2
Total Scenes: 952		
Reels: 10		

CARRY ON SCREAMING - 1966

Fenella Fielding in her second film, playing along side Harry H Corbett who was paid £12,000 for his only role in a Carry On. This film is a spoof of the popular Hammer Horror of the 1960s. A brilliant film with Kenneth Williams "frying tonight". This film is the longest running of the entire series at 97 minutes and is one of the people's favourites.

Data	Main Team Billings	Production Staff
Film: Colour	1. Kenneth Williams	Male: 18
Format: Feature Film	2. Jim Dale	Female: 3
Standard Projection: 24 fps	3. Charles Hawtrey	
Running Time: 1 hr 37 mins	4. Joan Sims	Film Started: Jan 1966
Gauge: 35mm	5. Peter Butterworth	Film Finished: Feb 1966
Aspect Ratio: 1.75	6. Bernard Bresslaw	Film Released: Aug 1966
Certificate: A		Locations Used: 3
Total Scenes: 816		
Reels: 10		

CARRY ON DON'T LOSE YOUR HEAD - 1966

Some of the location shots for this film took place at Waddenson Manor about six miles from Aylesbury in Buckinghamshire. Based around the French Revolution involving the aristocrats and royalists, with excellent performances from Williams as Citizen Camembert whose watchword was "every five minutes a sliced loaf", Sid James as The Black Fingernail who left his mark, Jim Dale as Lord D'Arcy and Peter Butterworth as Citizen Bidet. This was the thirteenth film in the series and certainly not unlucky for some!

Data	Main Team Billings	Production Staff
Film: Colour	1. Sid James	Male: 18
Format: Feature Film	2. Kenneth Williams	Female: 3
Standard Projection: 24 fps	3. Jim Dale	
Running Time: 1 hr 30 mins	4. Charles Hawtrey	Film Started: Sept 1966
Gauge: 35mm	5. Joan Sims	Film Finished: Oct 1966
Aspect Ratio: 1.75	6. Peter Butterworth	Film Released: Dec 1966
Certificate: A		Locations Used: 5
Total Scenes: 1,039		
Reels: 9		

CARRY ON FOLLOW THAT CAMEL - 1967

Follow that Camel was the second film under the Rank Organisation banner and the fourteenth of the series. It saw the one-off appearance of American actor Phil Silvers, famous as Sergeant Bilko. He was paid £30,000 for his role as Sergeant Ernie Nocker, equalling the fee paid to Elke Sommer for *Behind* in 1975, making them the highest paid actors of the series, though neither appeared in another Carry On. The locations for scenes were filmed in the sand dunes of Camber Sands, Rye, West Sussex, where the team spent three weeks filming, the longest of any spent on location.

Data	Main Team Billings	Production Staff
Film: Colour	1. Jim Dale	Male: 16
Format: Feature Film	2. Peter Butterworth	Female: 3
Standard Projection: 24 fps	3. Kenneth Williams	
Running Time: 1 hr 35 mins	4. Charles Hawtrey	Film Started: May 1967
Gauge: 35mm	5. Joan Sims	Film Finished: June 1967
Aspect Ratio: 1.75	6. Bernard Bresslaw	Film Released: Sep 1967
Certificate: A		Locations Used: 4
Total Scenes: 1,076		
Total Scenes Used: 216		
Reels: 10		

CARRY ON FOLLOW THAT CAMEL - 1967

Listed below is a breakdown of where and how many scenes were shot

Date	Pinewood stage/location	Number of scenes
2.5.67	Location (Camber Sands)	4
3.5.67	Location (Camber Sands)	11
4.5.67	Location (Icklesham)	4
5.5.67	Location (Camber Sands)	5
6.5.67	Location (Camber Sands)	11
7.5.67	Location (Camber Sands)	9
8.5.67	Location (Camber Sands)	16
9.5.67	Location (Camber Sands)	7
10.5.67	Location (Camber Sands)	13
11.5.67	Location (Camber Sands)	6
12.5.67	Location (Camber Sands)	6
13.5.67	Location (Camber Sands)	2
15.5.67	Location (Camber Sands)	5
16.5.67	Location (Camber Sands)	10
17.5.67	Location (Camber Sands)	7
19.5.67	H	4
22.5.67 (Strike over)	H & F	11
23.5.67 (Rain delay)	Lot	5
24.5.67 (Rain delay)	Lot	3
25.5.67 (Rain delay)	Lot	6
26.5.67	H	4
30.5.67	F	5
31.5.67	H & Lot	7
1.6.67 (Bad light)	Lot	2
2.6.67	Lot	9
5.6.67	Lot	9
6.6.67	Lot	11
7.6.67	F	3
8.6.67	F & H	3
9.6.67	H & F	4
12.6.67	F	4
13.6.67	F	5
14.6.67	Location (Swankleys)	2
15.6.67	Location (Swankleys) & F	4
16.6.67	F	4
19.6.67	Location (Osterley Park)	7
21.6.67	H	3
22.6.67	H & F	6
23.6.67	Lot & H	11

CARRY ON DOCTOR - 1967

The legendary Frankie Howerd joined the Carry On team for the first time as Francis Bigger bringing in his oohs and ahs. He appeared to fit in very well with his brand of comedy, and though he only appeared in two films he was considered a regular by many fans. Maidenhead Town Hall was used as the exterior of the hospital. Now midway through the series, the films were still growing in popularity. Sid James spent most of the film in bed, as this was his first role back after suffering a heart attack.

Data	Main Team Billings	Production Staff
Film: Colour	1. Kenneth Williams	Male: 16
Format: Feature Film	2. Sid James	Female: 3
Standard Projection: 24 fps	3. Charles Hawtrey	
Running Time: 1 hr 34 mins	4. Jim Dale	Film Started: Sept 1967
Gauge: 35mm	5. Hattie Jacques	Film Finished: Oct 1967
Aspect Ratio: 1.75	6. Peter Butterworth	Film Released: Dec 1967
Certificate: A	7. Bernard Bresslaw	Locations Used: 2
Total Scenes: 806	8. Barbara Windsor	
Reels: 10	9. Joan Sims	

CARRY ON UP THE KHYBER - 1968

This film, along with *Cleo*, appeared in the top 100 British films ever made. One of the costume greats of the series, it was the only time the team ventured out of England, to Snowdonia, North Wales, to film the 'Khyber Pass'. It was obviously an excellent choice, as an old friend of Peter Rogers phoned him after seeing the film to say that he had recognised part of the area as a part of India he had stayed in while serving in the army. This film is most people's favourite film of the series.

Data	Main Team Billings	Production Staff
Film: Colour	1. Sid James	Male: 18
Format: Feature Film	2. Kenneth Williams	Female: 3
Standard Projection: 24 fps	3. Charles Hawtrey	
Running Time: 1 hr 28 mins	4. Joan Sims	Film Started: Mar 1968
Gauge: 35mm	5. Bernard Bresslaw	Film Finished: May 1968
Aspect Ratio: 1.75	6. Peter Butterworth	Film Released: Aug 1968
Certificate: A	7. Terry Scott	Locations Used: 1
Total Scenes: 992		
Reels: 10		

CARRY ON CAMPING - 1968

This film, with *Screaming* and *Up The Khyber,* is in the top three of the Carry Ons. Set in the Paradise Campsite it brings out the fun of outdoor life, so put up your pole, and don't forget "beds up first, bunk up later". The filming took place in October/November and it was made to look like summer by spraying the grass with green paint. *Camping* is one of the funniest, with jokes coming thick and fast. Undoubtedly one of Rothwell's finest.

Data
Film: Colour
Format: Feature Film
Standard Projection: 24 fps
Running Time: 1 hr 28 mins
Gauge: 35mm
Aspect Ratio: 1.75
Certificate: A
Total Scenes: 907
Total Scenes Used: 177
Reels: 10

Main Team Billings
1. Sid James
2. Kenneth Williams
3. Joan Sims
4. Charles Hawtrey
5. Terry Scott
6. Barbara Windsor
7. Bernard Bresslaw

Production Staff
Male: 16
Female: 3

Film Started: Oct 1968
Film Finished: Nov 1968
Film Released: Feb 1969
Locations Used: 8

CARRY ON AGAIN DOCTOR - 1969

The eighteenth film in the series and the introduction of Patsy Rowlands into the Carry On team. Jim Dale as Dr Nookie who struck gold when he came across Gladstone Screwer in the Beatific Islands and came back with a weight-reducing serum and went into partnership with Ellen Moore (Joan Sims) to create the Moore-Nookie clinic. Jim Dale actually did his own stunts, and in the scene where he was on the hospital trolley going down the stairs he ended up in a real hospital, breaking a bone in his arm.

Data
Film: Colour
Format: Feature Film
Standard Projection: 24 fps
Running Time: 1 hr 29 mins
Gauge: 35mm
Aspect Ratio: 1.75
Certificate: A
Total Scenes: 868
Reels: 10

Main Team Billings
1. Sid James
2. Jim Dale
3. Kenneth Williams
4. Charles Hawtrey
5. Joan Sims
6. Barbara Windsor
7. Hattie Jacques
8. Patsy Rowlands
9. Peter Butterworth

Production Staff
Male: 15
Female: 3

Film Started: Mar 1969
Film Finished: May 1969
Film Released: Aug 1969
Locations Used: 4

CARRY ON CAMPING - 1968

A breakdown of how many scenes were shot, and where, people's favourite film

Date	Pinewood Stage/Location	Number of scenes
7.10.68	Lot (Orchard)	4
8.10.68	North Tunnel	7
9.10.68	Lot	7
10.10.68	Lot	5
11.10.68	Lot & North Tunnel	8
14.10.68	Lot	4
15.10.68	Lot	7
16.10.68	Lot & North Tunnel	7
17.10.68	Lot	9
18.10.68	North Tunnel	5
21.10.68	Lot	9
22.10.68	Lot	8
23.10.68	C	9
24.10.68	Lot & C	12
25.10.68	Lot & C	9
28.10.68	C	5
29.10.68	Club House & Gardens	4
30.10.68	C & Location (Northolt)	2
31.10.68	C & Location (Northolt)	2
1.11.68	C & Location (Northolt)	3
4.11.68	Location (Northolt)	6
5.11.68	Lot	3
6.11.68	Lot	4
7.11.68	C	5
8.11.68	C	8
11.11.68	C	3
12.11.68	Location (Burnham Beeches)	7
13.11.68	Location (Burnham Beeches)	5
14.11.68	Location (A412 & Courts) & Lot	8
15.11.68	Location (Pinewood Green Estate)	4
18.11.68	C	9
19.11.68	C	(1 night)
20.11.68	C & Location (Pinewood cul-de-sac)	3
21.11.68	A	8
22.11.68	A	1

CARRY ON UP THE JUNGLE - 1969

This film was Frankie Howerd's second and final Carry On. Almost entirely filmed at Pinewood Studios with the use of wildlife footage, this was not the king of the jungle for most fans. This film was one of the five that stalwart Kenneth Williams did not appear in. A fine performance from newcomer Jacki Piper and Terry Scott as Tarzan.

Data
Film: Colour
Format: Feature Film
Standard Projection: 24 fps
Running Time: 1 hr 29 mins
Gauge: 35mm
Aspect Ratio: 1.75
Certificate: A
Total Scenes: 1,048
Reels: 10

Main Team Billings
1. Sid James
2. Charles Hawtrey
3. Joan Sims
4. Kenneth Connor
5. Bernard Bresslaw
6. Terry Scott

Production Staff
Male: 15
Female: 3

Film Started: Oct 1969
Film Finished: Nov 1969
Film Released: Mar 1970
Locations Used: 2

CARRY ON LOVING - 1970

Now two-thirds of the way through the series, *Loving* was filmed on location in Park Street, Windsor, where the Wedded Bliss agency was situated, run by Sid and Hattie. The final scene brings out the good old slapstick custard pie in the face routine - and real cream was used. The scene was subsequently re-created for the Bounty advertisement on television.

Data
Film: Colour
Format: Feature Film
Standard Projection: 24 fps
Running Time: 1 hr 28 mins
Gauge: 35mm
Aspect Ratio: 1.75
Certificate: A
Total Scenes: 1,044
Total Scenes Used: 262
Reels: 10

Main Team Billings
1. Sid James
2. Kenneth Williams
3. Charles Hawtrey
4. Hattie Jacques
5. Joan Sims
6. Bernard Bresslaw
7. Terry Scott
    8. Patsy Rowlands
9. Peter Butterworth

Production Staff
Male: 17
Female: 3

Film Started: Apr 1970
Film Finished: May 1970
Film Released: Sep 1970
Locations Used: 6

CARRY ON HENRY - 1970

One of the all-time historical greats of the series, where Henry was renowned for chasing the women with his choppers, Sid James's famous phrase "Inn it again" was used when he fell into a pile of manure after being chased by a wench's father, played by Derek Francis. It was on the set of *Henry* that scriptwriter Talbot Rothwell was caught by Eamon Andrews with the big red book for *This Is Your Life*.

Data
Film: Colour
Format: Feature Film
Standard Projection: 24 fps
Running Time: 1 hr 29 mins
Gauge: 35mm
Aspect Ratio: 1.75
Certificate: A
Total Scenes: 992
Reels: 10

Main Team Billings
1. Sid James
2. Kenneth Williams
3. Charles Hawtrey
4. Joan Sims
5. Terry Scott
6. Barbara Windsor
7. Kenneth Connor
8. Peter Butterworth
9. Patsy Rowlands

Production Staff
Male: 17
Female: 3

Film Started: Oct 1970
Film Finished: Nov 1970
Film Released: Feb 1971
Locations Used: 3

CARRY ON AT YOUR CONVENIENCE - 1971

Originally called *Carry On Around the Bend* this classic saw the management versus the workers, which led to the strikes seen in this era. Brighton was used as the location for the factory's works outing, with Kenneth Cope making the first of his two Carry On appearances. He is trying to win over Jacki Piper but loses out to the new young star Richard O'Callaghan. Kenneth also loses his trousers outside the Odeon Cinema in Uxbridge; sadly the cinema is no longer there. A fire in 2003 destroyed the West Pier at Brighton where some of the scenes were shot for this film.

Data
Film: Colour
Format: Feature Film
Standard Projection: 24 fps
Running Time: 1 hr 30 mins
Gauge: 35mm
Aspect Ratio: 1.75
Certificate: A
Total Scenes: 1,043
Reels: 10

Main Team Billings
1. Sid James
2. Kenneth Williams
3. Charles Hawtrey
4. Hattie Jacques
5. Joan Sims
6. Bernard Bresslaw
7. Patsy Rowlands

Production Staff
Male: 17
Female: 3

Film Started: Mar 1971
Film Finished: May 1971
Film Released: Dec 1971
Locations Used: 5

CARRY ON MATRON - 1971

The last of the medical Carry Ons, *Matron*, the twenty-third film of the series brings out an excellent performance from Kenneth Williams as the hypochondriac Sir Bernard Cutting - the overall top team member in number of films appeared in. Sid James and Bill Maynard dress in disguise to locate the whereabouts of the pills stored at Finisham Maternity Hospital. This film saw the departure of Jacki Piper after her two-year contract ended, but in came the new face of Jack Douglas. Mostly filmed on location in Ascot and Denham village close to Pinewood Studios.

Data
Film: Colour
Format: Feature Film
Standard Projection: 24 fps
Running Time: 1 hr 27 mins
Gauge: 35mm
Aspect Ratio: 1.75
Certificate: A
Total Scenes: 996
Total Scenes Used: 157
Reels: 10

Main Team Billings
1. Sid James
2. Kenneth Williams
3. Charles Hawtrey
4. Hattie Jacques
5. Joan Sims
6. Bernard Bresslaw
7. Barbara Windsor
8. Kenneth Connor
9. Terry Scott
10. Patsy Rowlands
11. Jack Douglas

Production Staff
Male: 17
Female: 4

Film Started: Oct 1971
Film Finished: Nov 1971
Film Released: May 1972
Locations Used: 4

The Church in Denham Village, used for the final scene in Carry On Matron, shot on 2nd November 1971 and released in 1972

CARRY ON ABROAD - 1972

Set in the half-finished Elsbels Palace Hotel in Spain, which of course was Pinewood Studios. The Carry On team creates mayhem as the hilarious holiday laughter comes thick and fast. The furthest they travelled to make this film was to Bagshot in Surrey, for the dirt road leading to Elsbels (some holiday destination). Peter Butterworth played a number of characters in the film, showing his versatility. Many of the stars again were hoping for sunny climates, but once more they were disappointed.

Data
Film: Colour
Format: Feature Film
Standard Projection: 24 fps
Running Time: 1 hr 28 mins
Gauge: 35mm
Aspect Ratio: 1.75
Certificate: A
Total Scenes: 1,066
Total Scenes Used: 262
Reels: 10

Main Team Billings
1. Sid James
2. Kenneth Williams
3. Charles Hawtrey
4. Joan Sims
5. Kenneth Connor
6. Hattie Jacques
7. Bernard Bresslaw
8. Barbara Windsor
9. Patsy Rowlands
10. Jack Douglas

Production Staff
Male: 17
Female: 2

Film Started: Apr 1972
Film Finished: May 1972
Film Released: Dec 1972
Locations Used: 4

65 High Street, Slough – location used as the Wundatours Shop in Carry On Abroad (1972)

The Security Block at Pinewood Studios used as the Elsbels Airport in Carry On Abroad (1972)

CARRY ON MATRON - 1971

*Listed below is a breakdown of where and how many scenes
were shot for this, the last medical comedy of the series.*

Date	Pinewood stage/location	Number of scenes
11.10.71	B	7
12.10.71	B	4
13.10.71	B	5
14.10.71	B & A	6
18.10.71	A	7
20.10.71	A	10
21.10.71	A	4
22.10.71	A & B	4
25.10.71	B	5
26.10.71	Location (Ascot)	19
27.10.71	Location (Ascot)	13
28.10.71	B	4
29.10.71	B	10
1.11.71	B	2
2.11.71	B & Location (Denham)	11
3.11.71	B	8
4.11.71	A	8
8.11.71	A	4
9.11.71	A	6
10.11.71	A	10
11.11.71	A	3
12.11.71	A	7
15.11.71	A	3
16.11.71	A	2
17.11.71	A & Lot	8
18.11.71	North Tunnel	2
23.11.71	Theatre 5	1
25.11.71	Theatre 5	1
26.11.71	Theatre 5	1

CARRY ON GIRLS - 1973

Girls was the twenty-fifth of the series and again like *At Your Convenience* the team used Brighton for the location shoot as the fictitious town of Fircombe. Robin Askwith starred in his only Carry On film, after the success of the *Confessions* films. Well there were plenty to look at with Sid Fiddler and his beauty contest, and June Whitfield leads the movement to launch 'operation spoilsport' to halt it.

Data
Film: Colour
Format: Feature Film
Standard Projection: 24 fps
Running Time: 1 hr 28 mins
Gauge: 35mm
Aspect Ratio: 1.75
Certificate: A
Total Scenes: 1,169
Total Scenes Used: 131
Reels: 10

Main Team Billings
1. Sid James
2. Barbara Windsor
3. Joan Sims
4. Kenneth Connor
5. Bernard Bresslaw
6. Peter Butterworth
7. Jack Douglas
8. Patsy Rowlands

Production Staff
Male: 18
Female: 3

Film Started: Apr 1973
Film Finished: May 1973
Film Released: Nov 1973
Locations Used: 7

CARRY ON DICK - 1974

This was the last film for trio Sid James, Barbara Windsor and Hattie Jacques - a masterful performance from them all. One of the greats of the series with the Bow Street Runners after 'Big Dick'. After this film the Carry Ons appeared to be declining in popularity, and with the loss of three major team members the end was nigh.

Data
Film: Colour
Format: Feature Film
Standard Projection: 24 fps
Running Time: 1 hr 31mins
Gauge: 35mm
Aspect Ratio: 1.75
Certificate: A
Reels: 10

Main Team Billings
1. Sid James
2. Kenneth Williams
3. Barbara Windsor
4. Hattie Jacques
5. Bernard Bresslaw
6. Joan Sims
7. Peter Butterworth
8. Kenneth Connor
9. Jack Douglas
10. Patsy Rowlands

Production Staff
Male: 22
Female: 5

Film Started: Mar 1974
Film Finished: Apr 1974
Film Released: July 1974
Locations Used: 8

CARRY ON GIRLS - 1973

Listed below is a breakdown of where and how many scenes were shot in this, the second of the Brighton location films

Date	Pinewood stage/location	Number of scenes
16.4.73	Location (Brighton)	2
17.4.73	Location (Brighton)	8
18.4.73	Location (Brighton)	5
19.4.73	E	3
24.4.73	E	11
25.4.73	E	6
26.4.73	E	1
27.4.73	E	3
30.4.73	E	1
1.5.73	E	2
2.5.73	E	8
3.5.73	E	6
4.5.73	E	20
7.5.73	E	5
8.5.73	E	7
9.5.73	E & C	3
10.5.73	C	12
11.5.73	C	5
14.5.73	E	3
15.5.73	Location (Madeira Drive Brighton)	6
16.5.73	Location (Windsor) & E	7
17.5.73	Location (B410 & Slough)	5
18.5.73	E	3
21.5.73	E	7
22.5.73	E	2
23.5.73	E	3
24.5.73	E	3

CARRY ON BEHIND - 1975

The last of the great Carry Ons. In this film they returned to the same field where they filmed *Camping* some seven years earlier. It came complete with a talking mynah bird uttering the naughty words "Show us your knickers" and upsetting the campers. The voice for the bird was none other than Gerald Thomas, director of all the Carry On films. The scriptwriter for this film was Dave Freeman, taking over from Talbot Rothwell - a tough act to follow, but Dave managed it very well.

Data
Film: Colour
Format: Feature Film
Standard Projection: 24 fps
Running Time: 1 hr 30 mins
Gauge: 35mm
Aspect Ratio: 1.75
Certificate: A
Total Scenes: 1,138
Reels: 10

Main Team Billings
1. Kenneth Williams
2. Bernard Bresslaw
3. Kenneth Connor
4. Joan Sims
5. Jack Douglas
6. Peter Butterworth
7. Patsy Rowlands

Production Staff
Male: 15
Female: 3

Film Started: Mar 1975
Film Finished: Apr 1975
Film Released: Dec 1975
Locations Used: 6

CARRY ON ENGLAND - 1976

The second time the Carry On team visited the army barracks in their eighteen-year run. Filmed at Pinewood, it starred Windsor (Lovely Boy) Davies in his second and final Carry On. The men and women of the camp could not keep their hands of each other and even took to tunnelling into each other's barracks. Melvyn Hayes teamed up again with Windsor Davies for this film, as they appeared in *It Aint Half Hot Mum* together.

Data
Film: Colour
Format: Feature Film
Standard Projection: 24 fps
Running Time: 1 hr 29 mins
Gauge: 35mm
Aspect Ratio: 1.75
Certificate: A
Total Scenes: 935
Reels: 9

Main Team Billings
1. Kenneth Connor
2. Jack Douglas
3. Peter Butterworth
4. Joan Sims

Production Staff
Male: 20
Female: 4

Film Started: May 1976
Film Finished: June 1976
Film Released: Oct 1976
Locations Used: 1

CARRY ON EMMANNUELLE - 1978

This was film number thirty in a twenty-year span of Carry Ons. By now they had seemed to lose their way. Kenneth Williams played Emile Prevert putting on a French accent, which really wasn't him. Suzanne Danielle starred in her only Carry On as the sex-starved wife of Emile. Only a few members of the team starred in this film and, with the exception of *Columbus* fourteen-years later, the series was as good as finished. What a shame!

Data
Film: Colour
Format: Feature Film
Standard Projection: 24 fps
Running Time: 1 hr 28 mins
Gauge: 35mm
Aspect Ratio: 1.75
Certificate: AA
Reels: 10

Main Team Billings
1. Kenneth Williams
2. Kenneth Connor
3. Jack Douglas
4. Joan Sims
5. Peter Butterworth

Production Staff
Male: 20
Female: 4

Film Started: Apr 1978
Film Finished: May 1978
Film Released: Nov 1978
Locations Used: 6

CARRY ON MEMORY ...

"I was only in two Carry On films, which were *Loving* and *Girls*.
I cannot remember much about filming the Carry Ons, it's only when people say that they saw me in a Carry On the other night that I remember I did them, as it was just another job. Everyone was very professional. There was a low budget on them and you just had to get on as quickly as you could so that the finished product would come in on time."
- Bill Pertwee

CARRY ON COLUMBUS - 1992

After a fourteen-year break, they were back with the thirty-first film. *Columbus* was chosen to celebrate 500 years since he discovered America. Only Jim Dale and Jack Douglas remained from the original team, although Leslie Phillips played a cameo role thirty-three years after appearing in *Constable*. Bernard Cribbins also appeared, twenty-eight years since he last appeared in *Spying*. Another recognisable face was that of June Whitfield who was last seen in 1973 in *Girls*. It was nice to know that they all still liked to appear in the Carry Ons. June Whitfield once said in 1998 in the documentary *What a Carry On,* "They should have called it Carry Off Columbus." The reason why it did not work was that comedians tried to take the place of comedy actors. With so many now gone to the Carry On in the sky, they will never be repeated, though the films remain to this day Britain's biggest comedy film series export.

Data	Main Team Billings	Production Staff
Film: Colour	1. Jim Dale	Male: 58
Format: Feature Film	2. Jack Douglas	Female: 24
Standard Projection: 24 fps		
Running Time: 1 hr 31 mins		Film Started: Apr 1992
Gauge: 35mm		Film Finished: May 1992
Aspect Ratio: 1.75		Film Released: Oct 1992
Certificate: PG		Locations Used: 1
Reels: 10		

CARRY ON MEMORY ...

"A lovely memory from *Carry On Nurse* was as a hospital visitor under the eagle eye of Hattie Jacques the matron. I was measuring up my film husband Brian Oulton in his bed for his woolly jumper, which I was knitting for him, creating much embarrassment and giggles! Also in *Carry On Constable* outside the ladies loo on Ealing Broadway I remember asking PC Kenneth Connor for change of a penny - I was dying to go! It was grand working with such a brilliant team."
- Hilda Fenemore

APPENDIX 1
CARRY ON BOOKS & RELATED BOOKS

* *On the Way I Lost It*, Frankie Howerd (W H Allen 1976)
* *The Carry On Book*, Kenneth Eastaugh (David & Charles 1978)
* *Just Williams – An Autobiography*, Kenneth Williams (J M Dent 1985)
* *What A Carry On – The Offical Story of the Carry On Film Series*, Sally & Nina Hibbin (Hamlyn 1988)
* *Kenneth Williams*, Michael Freedland (Weidenfeld 1990)
* *Barbara – The Laughter and Tears of a Cockney Sparrow*, Barbara Windsor (Century 1990)
* *Titter Ye Not! – The Life of Frankie Howerd*, William Hall (Grafton 1992)
* *The Kenneth Williams Diaries*, Russell Davies (Harper Collins 1993)
* *The Kenneth Williams Letters*, Russell Davies (Harper Collins 1994)
* *Sid James*, Cliff Goodwin (Century 1994)
* *The Carry On Quiz Book*, Graham C Bromwich (Laid Back 1996)
* *Carry On Laughing – A Celebration*, Adrian Rigelsford (Virgin 1996)
* *The Carry On Companion*, Robert Ross (Batsford 1996 & 1998)
* *The Carry On Again & Quiz Book*, Graham C Bromwich (Laid Back 1998)
* *Carry On Uncensored*, Morris Bright & Robert Ross (Boxtree 1999)
* *High Spirits*, Joan Sims (Partridge Press 2000)
* *Frankie Howerd – The Illustrated Biography*, Mick Middles (Headline 2000)
* *The Life and Works of Peter Rogers*, Morris Bright & Robert Ross (BBC 2000)
* *All of Me – My Extraordinary Life*, Barbara Windsor (Headline 2000)
* *The Lost Carry Ons*, Morris Bright & Robert Ross (Virgin 2000)
* *And June Whitfield*, June Whitfield (Bantam 2000)
* *The Complete Sid James*, Robert Ross (Reynolds & Hearn Ltd 2000)
* *The Complete Frankie Howerd*, Robert Ross (Reynolds & Hearn Ltd 2001)
* *Charles Hawtrey, "The Man who was Private Widdle"*, Roger Lewis (Faber & Faber 2001)
* *A Twitch in Time: Jack Douglas' Life Story*, Sue Benwell (Able 2002)
* *Carry On Films*, Mark Campbell (Pocket Essentials 2002)
* *The Carry On Story in Pictures*, Robert Ross (Reynolds & Hearn 2005)
* *The Complete A to Z of Everything Carry On*, Richard Webber (Harper Collins 2005)
* *The Official Carry On Quiz Book*, Chris Cowlin and Paul Burton (Apex Publishing Ltd 2007)
* *No Laughing Matter*, Norman Hudis (Apex Publishing Ltd 2008)

APPENDIX 2
CARRY ON CLUBS & SOCIETIES

* *The British Comedy Appreciation Society*
'Laughter Lines', 1A Woodbury, Castle Road, Woking, Surrey, GU21 4ET
* *Cor! – The British Comedy Magazine*
24 Richmond Road, Basingstoke, Hampshire, RG21 5NX
* *The Hattie Jacques Appreciation Society*
34 Freemantle Avenue, Sutton Trust Estate, Hull, HU9 4RH
* *The Kenneth Williams & Sid James Society* (founded 1988)
"Stop Messin' About!", 27 Brookmead Way, Orpington, Kent, BR5 2BQ
* *The Grand Order of Newts Carry On Fanzine Magazine*
23 Braithwaite Drive, Colchester, Essex, CO4 5XG
* *Jack Douglas Headquarters*
RWCC, PO Box 19, Ventnor, PO38 1WD
* *The British Comedy Society*
28 Clarendon Road, Boreham Wood, Hertfordshire, WD6 1BJ
* *Carry On-Line website:* **www.carryonline.com**
13 Allingham Road, Reigate, Surrey, RH2 8JE
* *'Inn it Again'*
The Sid James Magazine, Svarttlonnheia 75, 4645 Nodeland, Norway
* *Carry On website* - **www.thewhippitinn.com**

CARRY ON MEMORY ...
"My memories of Carry On are very misty and obscure.
I did two of the films *Loving* and *At Your Convenience* - small
contributions amounting to about 2/3 days in total. I do remember
a scene with Kenneth Williams who was very easy to work with -
amusing, but I thought underneath rather sad. He seemed strangely
not happy about what he was working on, a nice man but ... that's
the only thing I took away from it all. All this took place in the
early 70s so it's not surprising it's a bit misty!"
- *Philip Stone*

APPENDIX 3
CARRY ON MERCHANDISE

Classic Memorabilia is possibly the largest retailer of Carry On merchandise in the country. Their merchandise includes videos, DVDs, audio cassettes, books, memorabilia, autographs and much, much more. For Carry On and many other classic comedies, please visit the Classic Memorabilia website: **www.classic-memorabilia.co.uk** or send for further information to the following address: *Classic Memorabilia, 52 Dene Court Road, Solihull, West Midlands, B92 8RQ Email: enquiries@classic-memorabilia.co.uk*

CARRY ON MEMORY ...

I was in four of the Carry Ons. I enjoyed every minute and I was at Pinewood and very occasionally on location filming them. I have many personal memories of the amazing cast of comedy actors, sadly no longer with us and I can honestly say, not replaced. My personal favourites to work with were the two Kennys, Connor and Williams. What must never be forgotten is the sheer brilliance of Gerry Thomas, his ability to keep the studio alive and moving forward amidst all the laughter and I dare say anarchy. He was able to keep many an ego at bay. His greatest strength to me was his trust of his actors to bring their own ideas to the floor and mould them into what he really wanted. And it only took seconds. We hardly went more than two takes per scene.
- *Larry Dann*

CARRY ON MEMORY ...

"I only appeared briefly in one Carry On film which was *Cabby*. My memory is of a group of Japanese journalists coming onto the set at Pinewood and going absolutely crazy with delight when they spotted Kenneth Williams and Charles Hawtrey (especially Charlie!) - Gerald Thomas virtually had to throw them out before we could resume shooting. Would love to have seen the Carry Ons dubbed into Japanese - AH SO!"
- *Peter Byrne*

APPENDIX 4
AN EXAMPLE OF A DAILY PROGRESS REPORT IN THE PRODUCTION OF A CARRY ON FILM

Number: _____

Production: _____

Production Number: _____   Day: _____   Date: _____

Set(s): _____   Days on Set: _____   Stage: _____

Director: _____   Cameraman: _____

Picture commenced: _____

	Studio	Location
Unit call: _____ finished: _____ Camera schedule days _____		
Camera days to date _____		

	Footage				Screen Time			
	Picture		Sound		Studio		Location	
	Gross	Print	Gross	Print	mins	secs	mins	secs
Today								
Previous								
To date								

Colour – Stills

Produce	ref	published

Scenes

Total in script:	
Shot to date:	
Scene shot today:	
Schedule for tomorrow:	
Scene number tomorrow:	

Artistes

Contract	Daily Rate

Special Equipment:
Vehicle/Animals:
Remarks:

THE AUTHOR - KEVIN SNELGROVE

Kevin (right), with Carry On producer Peter Rogers

Kevin Snelgrove was born in 1960 in Frome, a small town in the countryside of East Somerset. He has been a fan of the Carry Ons since he was nine years of age, and is now considered one of the country's leading experts.

He has attended many Carry On events held at Pinewood Studios where he has made brief appearances with Carry On producer Peter Rogers and actor Jack Douglas.

Kevin has also worked as a consultant for *Carry On* publications and production companies making Carry On programmes for television.

REVIEWS

"Kevin Snelgrove is without a doubt the leading expert on the Carry On films... all serious fans should read his book."
- Richard Wilson (Carry On Columbus)

"This is one of the most comprehensive books on the subject of the Carry Ons. Every fact, figure and statistic is here. Beautifully set out in chronological order with every detail you can possible want."
- Ken Rock, British Society of Comedy Writers (President)

REVIEWS

*"When compiling my 'The Complete A-Z of Everything Carry On',
I found Kevin's book an extremely valuable source of reference. Kevin
has completed a sterling job in assembling a myriad of facts and
figures about the Carry On films."*
**- Richard Webber, Author of
'The Complete A-Z of Everything Carry On'**

*"The Carry On films are so popular that a book of statistics about
them will be deeply appreciated by their many fans and followers."*
- Nicholas Parsons OBE (Carry On Regardless)

REVIEWS

"An astonishing book! I'm bowled over at the mere thought of the effort involved in putting it together with such style and wit."
- Norman Hudis (Writer of the First Six Carry On Films)

"A perfect book for those who need to know how many feet of film there are in Carry On Henry, or what percentage of Carry On films started production in the month of October. This book isn't just anal, it's completely bonkers. A must for quiz fanatics everywhere."
- Nigel Planer (Carry On Columbus)

REVIEWS

"I guess I am in a position to give you a quote on Carry On Figures, as I was one of the first actresses to bear mine for real in a film. The facts are: I loved being in the film, and working with the people I worked with, Kenny Connor and Sidney James were two of the nicest people I ever met, and I consider myself so lucky I had the chance to work with them. Statistics: those films will go on until there are no figures or statictics in the universe. They are DEFINITIVE, as all round escapism, and ENTERTAINMENT for all the family - and I'm not sure we'll ever have anything like them again.
Kevin has spent much time compiling this book, a true gem and a must for any Carry On fan!"
- Linda Regan (Carry On England)

"The Official Carry On Facts, Figures & Statistics is extremely informative and interesting. A must for all Carry On fans!
In 2008 The Carry On Films celebrate their 50 year anniversary, having started way back in 1958. My first one was in 1968, Carry On Up the Khyber and led to me appearing in 5 others and a Christmas special. I never thought that 40 years on people would still have such fond memories of this fantastic, fun, film series and I feel great to have been a part of it."
- Valerie Leon, (Appeared in 6 Carry On Films)

REVIEWS

"What an amazing piece of research and information, I suppose people do want all that knowledge somewhere. How gob smacked Kenneth Williams would have been if he could know there was such a tome as yours going to be written in the future!
The great skill of the production team of the 'Carry On' films was that they were amazingly clever at casting. They chose people of personality who were very quick worker's and fine comedians in their own right."
- Rosalind Knight (Carry On Nurse and Carry On Teacher)

"Everyone will love Kevin's book. I only did 'Carry On Sergeant' as I was working so much in the theatre, but I still wish I'd done more, they are so enjoyable to watch."
- Dora Bryan OBE (Carry On Sergeant)

REVIEWS

"Well done Kevin, How did he have the patience to get all those facts together? For anyone interested in film and of course the 'Carry On' fans will get a lot of fun from all of his hard work."
- Larry Dann (Carry On Teacher, Carry On Behind, Carry On England, Carry On Emmannuelle)

"I really enjoyed reading this book. It answers all the questions a Carry-On fan could possibly want to know and the little personal anecdotes from the cast are very amusing. It is a very welcome addition to any film-buff's library. It really is the definitive Carry-On reference work. Kevin has obviously been very diligent in putting together so many facts and figures."
- Valerie Van Ost (Carry On Cabby, Don't Lose Your Head, Doctor, Again Doctor)

REVIEWS

"I read and enjoyed the book. There was so much in it that I never knew about! I was a Supporting artist for 32 years and worked on over 800 productions but it was always fun to work on the Carry Ons ... I was always made to feel welcome by all the cast and crew and when I got to know Sid and Bernie, I'd sit in with them and play poker in between takes. I got to work with Babs (EastEnders) some years later and she was still nice. The films I worked on were: Camel, Khyber, Henry, Convenience, Abroad and Dick."
- **Harry Fielder (Supporting actor in 6 Carry On Films)**

REVIEWS

"The Official Carry On Book of Statistics by Kevin Snelgrove is a cornucopia of information - large trivial - about one of this country's greatest, and certainly most long-running, comedy exports. Everything you could possibly wish to know is here, the miscellany ranges from the fascinating (stars' dates of birth and birthplaces), the odd (films worked on over a specific period), and the mundane (vehicle registration plates). Kevin Snelgrove clearly knows his stuff, with basic lists such as stars and their Carry On appearances (broken down into number of scenes if you're interested), order of billing (in which the actors' popularity can be ascertained at a glance), and film locations (including distance travelled from Pinewood) easily the most interesting. Supporting actors are also given their due, with an extensive listing of pretty much everyone who has ever featured in a Carry On, even down to brief single appearances.

Sometimes, the facts are rather over-emphasised - such as a tally of Carry On films, TV shows and stage productions expressed as a list, as percentages, and again as a bar chart. It's easy to misinterpret some lists too, such as the ones for Big Three Scriptwriters and The Big Three Overall Scriptwriters, in which the same three writers have apparently differing scores.

But there's more than enough here to satisfy the most fact-hungry fan, with an especially exhaustive film-by-film listing at the back. On top of this, Snelgrove has assembled a great many Carry On actors to share their reminiscences, most of which shed new light on old stories, with almost all of them displaying huge affection for this iconic series."

- Mark Campbell, Author of 'Carry on Films:
The Pocket Essential Series'

REVIEWS

"Probably the most important Carry On fact, figure & statistic is that Kevin Snelgrove has researched his facts and figures meticulously, but his statistics leave a lot to be desired - and that is from someone who has seen him with the light on! Fascinating facts for any fan of the greatest film series ever made and mindboggling amusement for anyone who is discovering the Carry On's ... for the first time."
- Marc Sinden (Carry On Columbus)

"Here is the answer to that nightmare where you are one question away from the million pounds and it's a 'Carry On' related poser. An in-depth study of this book will prepare you for this moment and you thought it was simply a load of useless information. I pity you."
- Richard O'Brien (Carry On Cowboy)

REVIEWS

"Kevin's book bought back a hell of a lot of memories, and it made a very good read. My, oh my Kevin has done a lot of research that I would of never of thought of. So many of those wonderful characters that worked on the 'Carry On's' films with me are no longer with us, but never to be forgotten the crowd artist, stuntmen and women, and of course the stars of the show that made them household names."
- Nosher Powell (Carry On Dick)

"What a good idea and a very interesting reference book indeed. The Carry On films are, as we know, an institution and have become without a doubt a very important part of our British Comedy heritage. This book is a tribute to the hard work and resourcefulness of the excellent production teams and performers. I am sure Sid would have enjoyed reminiscing through the pages of facts and figures, well done Kevin, what a great deal of work you have done!"
- Valerie James (Wife of Sid James)

REVIEWS

"What a clever book - a fascinating feast of facts for all Carry On fans! I'm sure you will enjoy Kevin's book as much as I did."
- Jacki Piper (Carry On Matron, At Your Convenience, Loving, Up the Jungle)

"An excellent reference book for everything you ever wanted to know about the Carry on team. Some real little gems of information!"
- Steve Saville, Forest 92.3FM

REVIEWS

"There was a time when the only Carry On statistics I considered vital were 38-25-38 and related to Valerie Leon! Still, Kevin's pain-stakingly researched book continues to prove a great source of interest and amusement. Long may it Carry On ..."
- Robert Ross, Author of Various Carry On Books

"The Official Carry On Facts, Figures & Statistics is well presented and thoroughly researched. It will be hugely useful to all interested parties."
- Burt Kwouk (Carry On Columbus)

"I cannot imagine a more detailed book of information covering the 50 years of Carry On films. A treasure trove of facts and figures to delight the growing number of fans these films attract. I heartily applaud this mammoth statistical undertaking."
- Christine Ozanne (Carry on Nurse)

REVIEWS

"I love this book, I love all the detail, lists and other people's memories, they bring back all my own memories, which were very happy ones indeed."
- Fenella Fielding (Carry On Screaming and Carry On Regardless)

"Is it really 50 years since the first Carry On film, Sergeant in good old black and white, a truly classic film, which has stood the time. This fantastic book by Kevin, the shear time and effort to put together this minefield of facts and figures about the famous Carry On's. A must for all Carry On fans and people wanting to know about them. Carry On reading!"
- David Graham, The Heritage Foundation:
Film & Television Heritage

REVIEWS

*"I am amazed at the dedication, hours of hard graft and effort that has gone into compiling this book. Fans will read and enjoy.
Carry On reading!"*
**- Heather Emmanuel (Carry On Again Doctor
and Carry On Up The Jungle)**

"The Official Carry On Facts, Figures and Statistics is a great read. It is very well put together and a must read for Carry On Fans. I myself discovered so many facts I was not aware of although I was myself in Carry On Emmanuelle, playing the Doctor. Needless to say it was full of fun with Suzanne Daniel providing such a glamorous addition and Kenneth was at his element. I am glad that Kevin has put in so much details of all the films that the book will stay as a memorial for ever to all those involved in the series. I hope he will add on details of Carry On London as an addendum when the film is released."
- Albert Moses (Carry On Emmannuelle)

REVIEWS

"I was fascinated to see just how many facts and various statistics Kevin has managed to gather together for this book. Well done."
- Frank Thornton (Carry On Screaming!)

"I am still reeling from the amount of information, facts and figures your book contains. It must be the most comprehensive work of it's kind. The information you provide on the cost of the productions is in itself quite staggering. Even converting to today's money you would be hard put to mount an end of the pier show. Of course I only had a very minor roles to play in these films, with cameo parts in Don't Lose Your Head, Henry and At Your Convenience, but how I enjoyed playing them. Your book reminded me of how many of these wonderful films were made and how much I loved watching them."
- Leon Greene (Carry On Don't Lose Your Head, Henry and At Your Convenience)

REVIEWS

"This is a brilliant book that goes where no other Carry On related book has gone and leaves your head full of many a great Carry On related fact and figure! Buy now, increase your Carry On knowledge and be prepared to be amazed at the exhaustive research that Kevin has dedicated to this publication!"
- Paul Burton, Co-Author of 'The Official Carry On Quiz Book'

"Since watching Carry On Camping as a 10-year-old girl nothing since has ever seemed as funny. Terry Scott in his ridiculous long shorts (or were they short longs) ... Charles Hawtrey try just being ... well - Charles Hawtrey try and the inimitable Kenneth Williams being pursued by Hattie Jacques in his usual 'camp' manner ... Oh dear ... no pun intended ... As for double entendres ... they should just whip 'em out! I say, Carry on, Carry On films ... All carry on fans will enjoy this book!"
- Kate Robbins, Actress, Singer and Musician

REVIEWS

"For all those who love the Carry On films this book is a goldmine of information and can't fail to fascinate all who read it. To use Bernard's catch-phrase ..." I Only Asked" ... I think within the pages of this book lie many of the answers to the frequently asked questions about the Carry Ons and all who played a part in the successof the series."
- Liz Bresslaw, Wife of Bernard Bresslaw
(Appeared in 14 Carry On Films)

"This is an outstanding wee book with assets as plentiful as Mrs Pullitt's in their brief appearance in 'Carry On Matron'!"
- Madeline Smith (Carry On Matron)

"Unparelled! Unchangelled! If you need any statistic from the regime of the great Carry On films, you will undoubtly find it in Kevin Snelgrove's sparkling new book."
- Alan Curtis (Carry On Henry and Carry On Abroad)

REVIEWS

"I would say about my experience of working on the Carry on Columbus film was that it was such an enormous privilege and honour for a girl of my age then to be working with some of the best comic geniuses of our time. And also to be doing a film that was such a huge part of British comedy history. All Carry On fans should read this book."
- Holly Aird (Carry On Columbus)

"A statistician's dream, list opon list of facts you will be amazed Kevin has been able to find out. One of the world's most eccentric books. All, and more, than you wanted to know about the films that became cult classics, and spawned stage and TV spin-offs. Want to know the furthest distance travelled for location filming (the wilds of Snowdonia) or whether custard or cream was used in the slapstick "custard" pies? It's all here."
- Tina Rowe, Western Daily Press

OTHER CARRY ON PUBLICATIONS:

Published by Apex Publishing Ltd: www.apexpublishing.co.uk

The Official Carry On Quiz Book
Compiled by Chris Cowlin and Paul Burton, Foreword by Norman Hudis and Jacki Piper

ISBN 13: 978-1-904444-97-8   Price: £7.99

Who can forget the cheeky humour, outrageous characters and slapstick comedy that have characterised the 'Carry On' films over the last fifty years? Well, don't lose your head if you discover that the 1,000 questions in this quiz book highlight a few holes in your memory and you end up in hospital screaming for the saucy nurse and ending up with the grumpy old matron!

Covering every aspect of the 'Carry On' genre – the movies, release dates, characters, the stars and their lives, debuts, and much more – this book will propel you on a whirlwind journey from the Wild West to the Khyber Pass and every conceivable location in between, hotfooting through a range of historical eras, and jumping between black-and-white and Technicolor worlds.

Even if you find you're cruising on rough waters, carry on regardless, make the most of the entertainment facilities, delve into the treasure trove of facts and figures, and allow your fond recollections to turn your frowns into the smiles and giggles that encapsulate the 'Carry On' ethos.

OTHER CARRY ON PUBLICATIONS:

Published by Apex Publishing Ltd: www.apexpublishing.co.uk

No Laughing Matter: How I Carried On
By Norman Hudis, Foreword by Peter Rogers

ISBN 13: 978-1-906358-15-0   Price: £7.99

For the first time, in NO LAUGHING MATTER, Norman Hudis, who wrote the first six Carry On movies, reveals his hitherto secret, decades-long and quixotic writing-activity since he left the series. It's this: He Carried On Writing Carry On stories in the hope that, one day, he'd be asked to return and come up with one!

Two typical intriguing examples, elaborated in these memoirs: "Carry On Under The Pier If Wet", skewering two doughty British institutions, the seaside concert-party and boarding-house - and, most audacious of all, "Carry On Shylock Holmes."

More firsts revealed within these pages: Norman's frank and terse opinions about, among others, Ted Ray, Hattie Jacques, Joan Slms ("Did I sleep with her?"), Charles Hawtrey ("Do you believe in fairies?"), Kenneth Connor and Kenneth Williams and, in Hollywood, Elvis Presley, Robert Young, Anne Baxter, Erik Estrada, Joan Crawford and Harold Shmidlap ("Who's he?" Hint: legendary creator of the TV series "Frontier Accountant.")

Emerging, somewhat bewildered, but with a firm sense of comedy implanted in him by undergoing upbringing by a rather odd family, Norman felt compelled to seek substitute families to redress the balance: respectively as a young newspaperman, then serving airman in the WWII RAF, plus post-war film publicist and, finally, fully home, as a writer.

This autobiography, therefore, with a fitting foreword by Carry On producer Peter Rogers, is Norman Hudis in a succinct and delightful nutshell.

In his words: "I call the book NO LAUGHING MATTER as an understatement, because my life, beginning with the upbringing by my unconventional family, has actually been such a hysterical hoot, it's no great wonder that I write comedy. After all, let's face it, I've lived it."